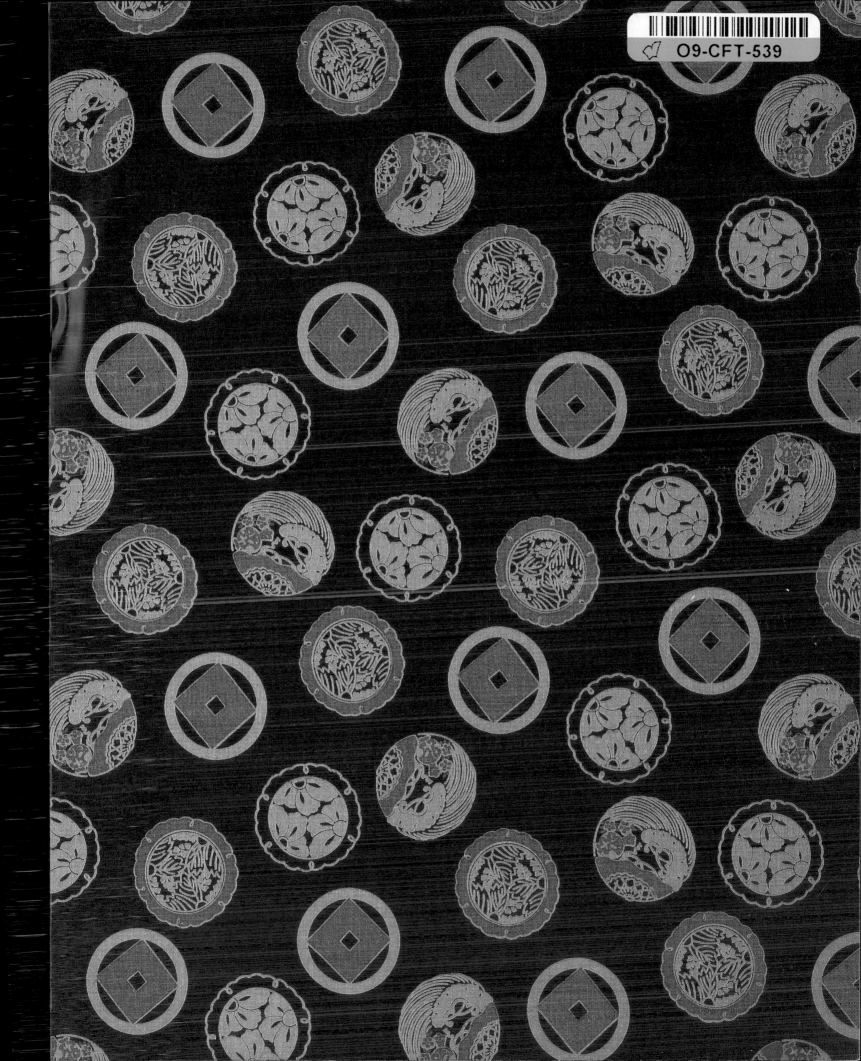

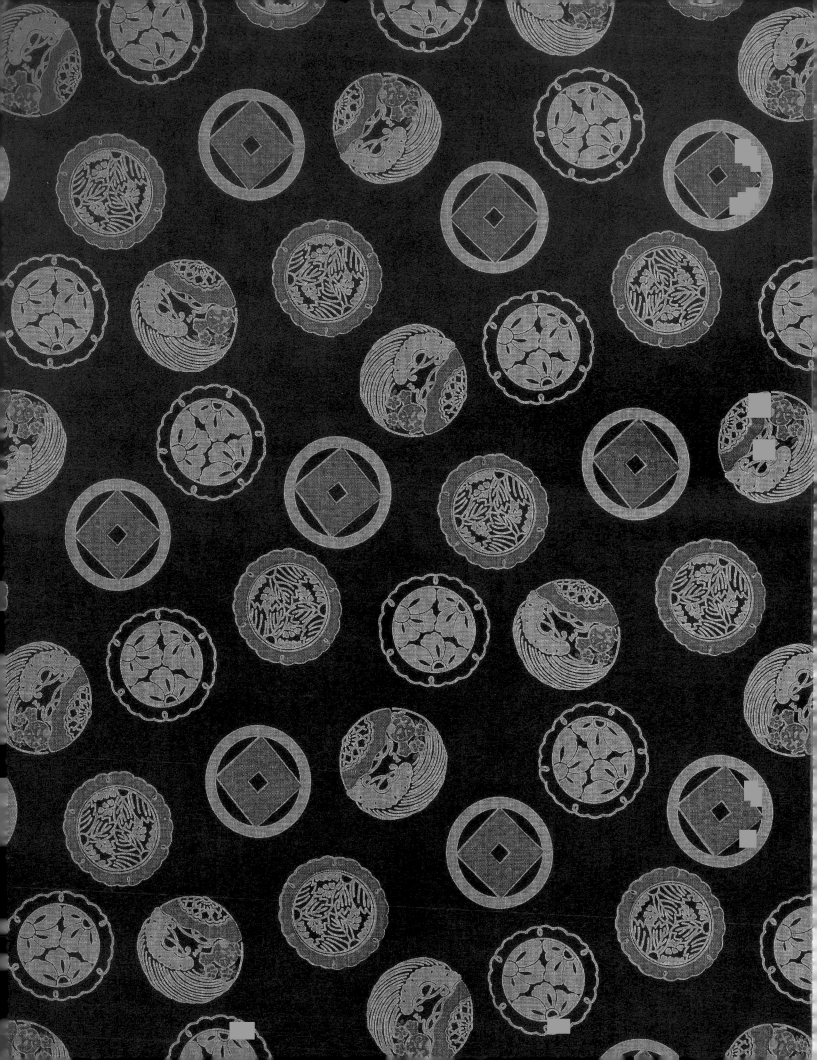

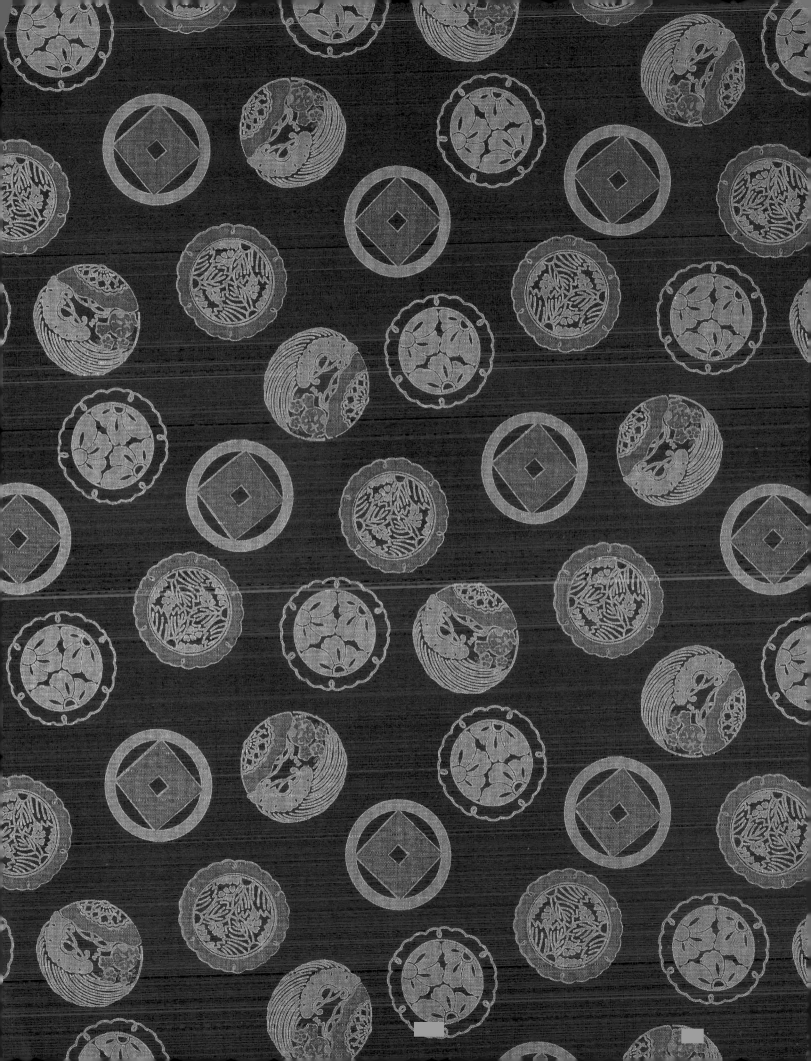

CIRCLES
of The East

Quilt Designs from Ancient Japanese Family Crests

Kumiko Sudo

THE QUILT DIGEST PRESS
NTC/Contemporary Publishing Company

Library of Congress Cataloging-in-Publication Data

Sudo, Kumiko.

 Circles of the East : quilt designs from ancient Japanese family crests / Kumiko Sudo.

   ISBN 0-8442-2657-2

   1. Patchwork—Patterns. 2. Quilting—Patterns. 3. Appliqué—Patterns.

   4. Crests—Japan.   I. Title.

   TT835.S789   1997

   746.46'041—dc21   97-2582

                                                                CIP

The author thanks Hoffman California Fabrics, Momen House Fabrics,

P&B Textiles, and Clover Needlecraft, Inc. for their support.

Editorial and production direction by Anne Knudsen.

Book design by John Lyle, San Francisco.

Cover design by Nick Panos.

Introduction by Kumiko Sudo with Mary Elizabeth Johnson.

Editing by Mary Elizabeth Johnson.

Technical editing by Randi Nervig.

Technical drawings by Kandy Petersen.

Manufacturing direction by Pat Martin

Quilt photography by Bill Bachhuber

Other photography by Sharon Hoogstraten, unless specifically credited.

Published by The Quilt Digest Press

An imprint of NTC/Contemporary Publishing Company

4255 West Touhy Avenue

Lincolnwood (Chicago), Illinois 60646-1975, U.S.A.

Printed in Singapore

International Standard Book Number: 0-8442-2657-2

Circles of the East is my tribute to
those ancient designers
who created these delicate
and detailed motifs,
perfectly contained in tiny circles.

Blocks and Quilts

Introduction

My father's crest was woven into his kimonos, *a plain
circle with two bars through it, representing dragons.*

Kamon—Japanese Family Crests

Surprisingly, it was not until I had been living in the United States for more than twelve years that I began to appreciate Japanese *kamon* or family crests. I was brought up in a very traditional Japanese home, where *kamon* were a natural part of everyday life. My mother's dishes were embellished with her family's crest, a lovely jacaranda blossom design. My father's crest was woven into his *kimonos*, a plain circle with two bars through it, representing dragons. The same crest was a part of our family altar. I accepted our crests and those of all the families I knew as symbols of the culture in which I grew up, and never investigated the tradition behind them nor the exquisite artistry of their design.

One of my favorite crest designs is the jacaranda blossom from my mother's family. Here, it is colorfully displayed on a vest. On marriage, though sometimes the two families combine crests, most often the wife adopts the husband's crest, and their children use his crest or a variation on it. Usually, the wife will bring items, particularly from her trousseau, into the marriage that are marked with her original family crest. Collection of Kumiko Sudo.

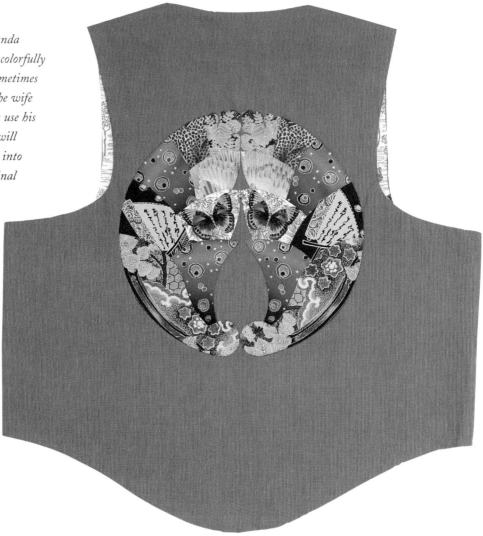

It was not until I began to research *Circles of the East* that I became reaquainted with *kamon*. It has brought me untold pleasure to explore, for the first time, the wonderful designs of artists who lived more than a thousand years ago and who left behind them a unique art form. *Kamon*, handed down through the ages from generation to generation, are intricately designed motifs, usually taken from nature, that sit perfectly within circles that can measure as small as an inch (2.5 cm) in diameter. By translating these tiny treasures into my own artistic medium of quilt design, my goal has been to share this relatively unknown Japanese decorative art with the rest of the world.

The Tradition of Kamon

The Japanese tradition of holding a *kamon*, or family crest, is as ancient as the revered tea ceremony. Still in use today, family crests are most often found on formal *kimonos* made of black fabric and worn on special occasions such as weddings, special birthdays, New Year's Day, and funerals. Mostly circles, these beautiful genological symbols number more than 5000 in all, and the history of how they came to be so ingrained in Japanese society is as fascinating as the individual stories behind each crest.

Crests and Country Intertwined

In Japanese history, the display of *kamon* was from earliest times a sign of status. The first record is found in the ancient court history Shoku Nihongi, which describes the use of a sun, moon, blue dragon, tortoise, white tiger, and a three-legged crow on the banners of the emperor Mommu in the year 701. All these motifs are Chinese emblems of great antiquity, as are the stylized cloud formation, crane, phoenix, and dragon that were used by the Japanese court as early as 704-784.[1]

In the latter part of the 400-year Heian period (794-1185), the nobles of the Japanese Imperial Court used these symbols, as well as other flowers and birds, to adorn the lacquered cow drawn carriages in which they rode. As the nobles traveled from their fiefdoms to the Imperial Court in Heian (present Kyoto), the decorations on the carriages became a means of distinguishing themselves on the often-crowded roadways. These simple symbols gradually evolved into intricately designed *kamon*. As time passed, the crests began to be used as decoration on the robes of the court nobles. Succeeding generations used the same symbols as a mark of ancestry and nobility.

During the wars that developed at the end of the Heian period, a practical, rather than decorative, use for crests came into being. Warriors needed precise signs to distinguish allies and enemies clearly in the middle of chaotic battlefields. The motifs they chose—arrows, hawk-feathers, serpents, and dragons—were completely different in spirit from the flowers and birds used by the court nobles.

[1] Dower, John W., *The Elements of Japanese Design*. Weatherhill, Inc. New York & Tokyo. 1971. pp 3–4.

The sails of ships made wonderful places to display kamon, *like this simple maple design. Ando Hiroshige, Japanese, 1797–1858,* Ferryboat at Arai, *woodcut, unknown. Gift of Mr. and Mrs. Harold G. Henderson, 1963.670. Photograph © 1997, The Art Institute of Chicago. All rights reserved.*

Japanese Historical Periods

Jomon (Neolithic)
c. 10,000 B.C. to c. 200 B.C.

Yayoi
c. 200 B.C. to c. 200 A.D.

Kofun (Tumulus)
200 to 593

Asuka
593 to 710

Nara
710 to 794

Heian
794 to 1185

Kamakura
1185 to 1333

Muromachi (Ashikaga)
1336 to 1573

Azuchi Momoyama
1573 to 1603

Edo (Tokugawa)
1603 to 1867

Meiji
1868 to 1912

Taisho
1912 to 1926

Showa
1926 to 1989

Heisei
1989 to Present

On kimono, *the circular crest design measures about one and a quarter inches (three and a half centimeters) for men, and about one inch (two and a half centimeters) for women. Woven in white, crests were traditionally displayed on the back of the kimono and on each sleeve. On very formal wear, additional crests were displayed on the front of each shoulder, making five crests in all. Less formal kimono have just one crest on the back. Collection of Kumiko Sudo.*

Ramon As Symbols of the Samurai

The Kamakura Period (1185-1333) saw the decline in influence of the noble class and the rise of a warrior class, known as the *bushi*, or *samurai*. It came into general fashion among soldiers to use heraldic symbols not only on their flags, but on their tents, helmets, shoulder-protectors, shields, and horse-armor. Toward the end of the period there was no influential family without its crest; those of the most celebrated clans or families were known to everyone. A folk tale tells of a clever soldier who avoided a surely fatal attack by a much larger force by having his handful of men hold aloft flags painted with the different crests of many powerful warriors, thereby fooling his enemy into thinking he was supported by a great host of soldiers. This ruse would not have worked later,

A feudal lord and his retainers stayed overnight at one of the fifty three stations between Edo and Kyoto. At dawn, they are almost ready for departure. Curtains and lanterns display the lord's family crest. From the woodblock print Departure at Dawn, *by Ando Hiroshige (1797-1858), from the series* Fifty-Three Stations of the Tokaido, *1833-34. Collection of Kumiko Sudo.*

The kimono *of this* Kabuki *actor bears an Imperial chrysanthemum crest. Ippitsusai Buncho, Japanese, 18th century, Segawa Kikunojo II as the courtesan Hitachi in Act 2 of* Wada Sakamori Osame no Mikume, *woodcut, unknown, gift of Miss Katherine S. Buckingham to the Clarence Buckingham Collection, 1925.2525. Photograph © 1997, The Art Institute of Chicago. All rights reserved.*

The Imperial Crest

It was during the early Kamakura Period (1185-1333) that the chrysanthemum was first used as a crest of the Imperial Court. Originally, the motif was used simply as decoration for clothing and furniture—non-official purposes—but by the end of the period, it was recognized as an Imperial crest, ranking in stature with the crest of the Sun and Moon, the first royal *kamon*. Reserved for the royal family, the Imperial crests were, at first, occasionally granted to those who rendered outstanding service to the court. However, this practice was dropped in later years, and, to this day, the Chrysanthemum is forbidden to anyone but the Imperial family.

as it eventually came to be that all the soldiers in a particular army marched under a single crest, usually that of their leader.

Honored crests were given to warriors who distinguished themselves in battle. People could tell who a soldier was and where he was from by looking at his crests. If his achievement was especially outstanding, a *samurai* could be awarded his commander's own family crest, a very high honor.

During the Muromachi period (1333-1573), increased contact between the warrier class and the court enhanced the soldiers' interest in fashion, so that, in addition to the decorations adopted for use on the battlefield, another set of crests came to be used for purely social occasions. It also became quite the rage among the *samurai* to select one of the purely decorative floral patterns of the court and intersperse sword blades among the petals. At the same time, the nobles decided to take on a more military air for themselves, discarding their palanquins for horses, their ceremonial robes for armor, and their traditional decorative family crests for ones that reflected more closely those of the warrior class. In spite of the great proliferation of family crests, the authors of military histories of the time seemed confident that their readers would know who was on which side by simply listing the markings on their banners.[2]

The martial class emerged as Japan's real ruler during the twelfth century, and the wars between feuding clans dragged on for the next three hundred years. During this time the country was divided into small domains, with the warrior kings, or *daimyo*, who ruled these fiefdoms sometimes staying in power for very brief periods. The constant warfare and changing fortunes had a complicating effect on heraldry: on the one hand, family crests changed rapidly as families rose and fell in power; on the other hand, visual symbols became even more important as a means of identifying who someone was and how he got to be in his position. It was a time of great inventiveness in design, and a time of the development of derivative crests, which were based in some way on the design of the senior crest of the family. However, there were almost no laws governing the design or use of crests, except that the right to use them was held only by the court and warrior classes of the nation, which represented at most only five to six percent of the population.

[2] *Ibid* p 8.

Kamon in Times of Peace

Peace was finally established after the victory of Tokugawa in 1600, marking the beginning the Edo Period, which lasted until 1867. During these nearly three hundred years of peace, society changed enormously. Military standards and tents practically went out of use; wealth and status became the cornerstones of society. Accordingly, the significance of family crests gradually changed from recognizing great war exploits to denoting family lineage and position. In 1642, nearly ten centuries after their first appearance in Japan, crests became loosely regulated by laws; certain symbols or variations thereof were allocated to certain families, and the use of these crests by anyone other than the designee was prohibited. However, the practice of transfering crests from one family to another made this rule difficult to enforce, and even those emblems set aside for the Imperial family were freely appropriated. However, once a certain crest was registered, no alterations could be made to it.

As the period of peace lengthened into centuries, the importance of crests evolved from ceremonial to decorative. The function of crests was enjoyed especially by the rising merchant class, who seemed to care little for the history associated with the wearing of crests, and saw them as motifs to be sprinkled liberally on their clothing. Sometimes a motif would be repeated to form the printed design of the fabric of a *kimono*; in other cases, a crest would be enlarged to a size that covered the entire *kimono*, so that only parts of the motif were visible on any one area of the garment.

Crests began to adorn a variety of other items. Powerful lords worked their crests into the palaces, castles, and temples they built—Edo castle was marked with the hollyhock of the Tokugawa family. *Daimyo* worked their family crests into roof tiles, gates, pillars, transoms, bells, and the stone lanterns of their estates. Buddhist temples and Shinto shrines were often marked with the family crests of those who had caused them to be built. Family crests were placed on tombstones, a tradition still in use. The sails of ships were perfect backgrounds for large family crests, visible to all as the lords from the southern islands made their periodic journeys to Edo by crossing the Inland Sea.

The European Heraldic Tradition

Emerging in the West at about the same time as family crests were adopted in the East, European heraldry developed during the eleventh and twelfth centuries. During the crusades, as knights from all over Europe began to travel to the Holy Lands in the Middle East, motifs were used to identify home countries and regions. Western heraldry is based for the most part on the animal kingdom. Lions, leopards, wolves, monkeys, wild boars, and eagles are joined by fantasy creatures like mermaids, dragons, and griffins. The garden is also represented in European heraldry, but not nearly so completely as in the Japanese tradition. Such floral devices as *fleur-de-lis* and the Tudor Rose, which combines the two colors of the English War of the Roses, are commonplace. Whereas the Japanese made no use whatsoever of the human form, European coats of arms frequently show parts of the body. Another big difference is the use of color. While Japanese crests are traditionally rendered in white on a black background, European coats of arms use up to seven colors: white, black, blue, yellow, red, green, and purple. Additionally, gold and silver embellish the designs.

The rice measure crest—three nesting measures—on this actor's kimono *belonged to the great line of Kabuki actors who descended from Ichikawa Danjuro. Katsukawa Shunsho, Japanese 1726-1792,* The Actor Ichikawa Danjuro IV in a Shibaraku Role, *woodblock print, c. 1770, Clarence Buckingham Collection, 1925.2365.*

The kimono *of the courtesan displays a family crest. Chobunsai Eishi, Japanese, 1756-1829,* Kumegawa of Ogi-ya House, *woodblock print c. 1793, Clarence Buckingham Collection, 1925.3111.*

Actors and licensed courtesans wore sumptuous costumes, embellished with crests of their own design, often elaborate and imaginative. Entertainers of the time held a remarkable sway over the public imagination, not unlike today, and the crests adopted by the most popular actors and the best-known courtesans came to be favored by young and old alike, many times in preference to their own family crests.

Kamon Come Full Circle

The purpose to which family crests were put had come full circle—back to the purely decorative. Household items, such as tables, chests of drawers, chopstick boxes, bowls, and wooden pillows bore a family's crest. Personal accessories like fans, combs, mirrors, and trousseau items were marked in much the same way as we would use monograms today. Eventually, consumer items such as bottles of sake, rice cakes, toys, and even toothpicks were provided with emblems, like trade monograms.

By the beginning of the Meiji Era (1868-1912), there was no limit at all on who could wear a family crest. All families could have them. As the twentieth century progressed, and as Western customs and costumes became popular in Japan, the practice of wearing crests declined considerably. However, cities continue to have their own family crests, and corporations use them as logotypes: the circular crane for Japan Air Lines, a plum blossom on plum wine. Crests are still a part of the theater, including *Noh* and *Bunraku* as well as *Kabuki*.

Even today, at the end of the twentieth century, it is rare that a native Japanese does not own a crested black *kimono* for those ceremonial occasions, no matter how little or how much money the family has, or how high or low their station in life. It is not uncommon for Japanese people to start a conversation with one another by asking, "What is your family crest?" Pleasant exchanges about each other's lineage and ancestors generally follow, allowing the participants to get to know one another more easily.

The elaborate design of this child's ceremonial kimono *includes delicate family crests on the back and the sleeves. This* kimono *is for a newborn. When parents and grandparents first take the child to a shrine about thirty days after its birth, the baby is held with the* kimono *draped over its back. Collection of Kumiko Sudo.*

The Design of Kamon

Japanese family crests demonstrate incredible variety and inventiveness that date back to ancient times. The vast majority of the designs come from the world of nature; some feature physical objects and others geometric forms. Motifs drawn from the animal world are comparatively few; birds and insects are favored over animals. A striking difference with European heraldry, neither man nor parts of the human anatomy appear at all in the mainstream of Japanese crests.

Although crests eventually became so popular as to be almost ubiquitous, their designers did not enjoy the same recognition, except, occasionally, through folklore. The designers of most crests remain anonymous, although their work ranks as some of the most creative and inventive graphic design of all civilization. Each crest design fulfills the aspiration of any designer: it is vigorous, full of meaning, arresting, and unforgettable. *Kamon* may even be said to represent the genius of the Japanese for stylized pattern.

Kamon occupy an esteemed place among the graphic arts of Japan. They never lost their function as pure design, and their symbolic connotations are generally appreciated throughout the country. Their potential for application to such fields as the design of wallpapers, floor coverings, mosaics, jewelry, and textiles, including quilts, has not been much exploited.

Crests within Perfect Circles

It is thought that the stylized patterns of the crests were influenced in part by an ancient design discipline in which the characters used for calligraphy were transformed into geometric designs. Tradition dictated that calligraphic designs must be made to fit perfectly within a square. The same discipline was behind the shaping of a motif into the circle most often used for family crests.

The circle has particular meaning in Oriental beliefs. A good example is the "whirl picture" formed by the comma-shaped *yin*-and-*yang* symbols that interlock to make a perfect circle. The whirl picture represents the union of the Heaven God and the Earth Goddess, of Light and Darkness; from that, the

This woman's summer kimono *is made from* ro
*fabric, a very fine silk gauze. It has a very unusual
color effect. There are five crests in all on the*
kimono, *of which three show in the image.*

circle itself came to symbolize the union of heaven and earth, or the cosmos. In Buddhism, the circle represents perfection. Further evidence of the significance of the circle in Japanese culture may be found in the perfect-circle stamps, carved from ivory or boxwood, that have traditionally been used to replace signatures done with pen and ink.

In the designing of crests, many motifs were stylized within the circle. Each motif bore a particular meaning: for example, bamboo, pine, iris, and tangerine symbolized good health and vitality. A gingko, pine cone, squash, butterfly, or nandina stood for continuation and prosperity. Cranes, turtles, and pine trees were for long life. Three wheels or pestles meant unity. A fan and *noshi* were required items when a celebration was in order. Cherry and plum were the symbols of elegance, and wisteria and butterflies promised prosperity.

Inspiration for the design of many crests was taken, no doubt, from the many pattern books published for use by craftsmen who worked with applied design, whether they were lacquering a box or printing a fabric. Some of these books were a compilation of one designer's work, but many were design dictionaries of popular motifs that had been used throughout time.[3] These compilations were the text-books for aspiring designers, who studied them assiduously as they went through an arduous basic training. They not only provided excellent examples for study, but encouraged the user to come up with new designs out of those already in existence. Another source for those seeking to design their own family emblem were the *kimono* makers, who kept records of family crests.

Flower Designs in Kamon

For many years, my mother taught the Japanese art of flower arrangement, so I grew up among flowers. Flowers are my best friends, and they are my mentors, leading me to my love of nature, which has always been an inspiration and a comfort to me. In choosing crest designs for *Circles of the East*, it has been natural for me to lean toward those that use a floral motif. Flowers have caught the imagination of the Japanese people since very early times, as more than half of the crests in existence use this powerful image.

[3] Three standard references are *Furyu Ezukushi (A Series of Fashionable Pictures)*, published in 1685; *Joyo Kimmo Zui (Pictorial Encyclopedia for Women)* published in 1687; and *Chinzoku Hinagata Miyako Fuzoku (Customs of the Capital, Models of Rare Colours)*, of 1716.

In the mid-sixth century, as Buddhism traveled from India through China into Japan, it brought with it motifs from Indian and Chinese decorative arts, some of which had their genesis in ancient Greece. But the greatest influence of Buddhism on Japanese crest design was the love of and reverence for nature that is a tenet of the religion.

An appreciation of flowers is evident from the songs, poems, and literature of the latter Heian Period (794-1185). It was about this time that an elegant pastime, the "flower comparison party," came into being. Each person brought a selection of flowers to the party, and the beauty of each was gently compared to others. This heightened awareness of the beauty of flowers accounts in no small part for the floral patterns that embellished clothing, household utensils, and various other articles of daily use, as well as for their abundance in Japanese crests.

With the introduction of tea seeds about 1100 years ago to Japan (via India through China), the tea ceremony became an integral part of the life of the nobility. Taking of tea nourished not only the body, but the spirit as well. At each ceremony, a special flower arrangement, specific to the nature of the group, was present. Each flower also has its own individual meaning, and the language they speak is an enduring element of Japanese culture.

An interesting note: one flower that was never used for a crest design is the hydrangea; it represents inconstancy.

Other Design Motifs

Though none was nearly as popular as flowers, the following motifs occur in crest design: natural objects, such as the sun, moon and stars, waves, animals, fish, birds, and insects; objects of human craftsmanship, such as bottles, bells, wheels, arrows, ships and rudders, fans, windmills, fishing nets, drums, ladders, and so on; geometrical patterns like the lozenge, diamond, interlocked rings, bars, and squares. It is clear from this short summary that almost anything can and has been the inspiration for a crest design. There are some 400 or so different categories of motifs, and some 5000 variations. To enjoy this incredible variety of design for yourself, examine some of the books listed in the Bibliography.

Originally, crests were designed in white on a black background, and they were usually painted onto or dyed into fabric. Occasionally, they were stiched in white, gold, or silver thread. During the innovative times of the Edo period, some designers tried coloring or tie-dyeing the motifs, but most returned to the traditional rendering of the crest in white on black, which is how they are most often seen today.

Color has always been an important part of my work as a fabric artist, as it is to all quilters. What I found most exciting when working with *kamon* was the opportunity to render these wonderful, delicate designs in color. For me, introducing color to these ancient symbols is a way of giving them new depth. It was a creative challenge that has allowed me to interpret the crests in a way that has meaning to me and that is visually pleasing.

I have also enlarged the crests to fill a quilt block from the smaller circles in which they were first created and are most often seen. This idea of enlarging a *kamon* is not original to me, though. It was practiced during the Edo period as shopkeepers used large family crests on signboards and shop curtains to identify themselves as sellers of *kimono*, *kanzashi* (hair accessories), or candle stands, for example. These days, you can see them at authentic Japanese restaurants, on theater stage curtains, or on ceremonial draperies and flags.

When you are planning what you will make, you should keep in mind that a motif the size of a quilt top will need a distance of at least ten feet (meters) from which to be viewed if one is to see the motif in its entirety; however, a single block that is fourteen or fifteen inches square (thirty-five or thirty-seven centimeters square) is easily seen and can be hung in almost any room. Though all the blocks in *Circles of the East* are hand-sewn, the larger motifs could also be put together with a sewing machine, if desired.

When it comes to deciding how to design a quilt, rather than a block, from one of the crest designs, there are several directions you can take. I have had success with multiples of

This decorative banner was used for Boy's Day celebrations, a May 5 holiday in Japan. Banners like this can still be seen in the countryside around Boy's Day. Collection of Kumiko Sudo.

16

one block (see page 32), also with rearranging the templates in the block to make unusual quilt designs (see page 56). I have experimented with enlarging just a portion of a *kamon* design and using it as a secondary motif, thereby following the Japanese tradition of using crest designs as a starting point to create new and fresh designs.

It was very difficult for me to limit *Circles of the East* to just thirty crest designs from the thousands that make up the tradition. My criteria for final selection became the artistic challenge that each individual design offered.

The more I study *kamon*, the more respect I have for those ancient designers who created such delicate and detailed motifs, perfectly contained in tiny circles. This book is my tribute to them.

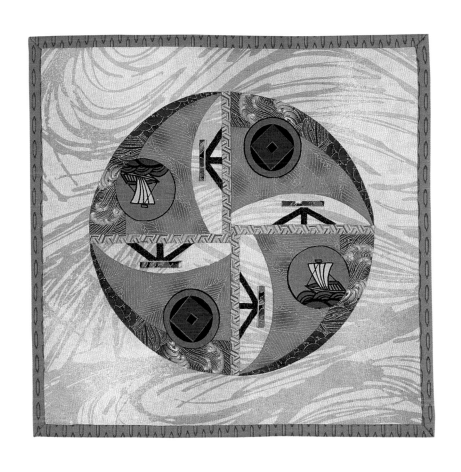

How to Use This Book

Thirty block designs based on Japanese family crests, including:

- A color photograph and diagram of each block
- Step-by-step diagrams for making each block
- Pattern templates for each block
- The story behind each crest design

Six quilt designs, including

- A color photograph of each quilt
- Step-by-step construction instructions with drawings
- Fabric requirements

A total of thirty designs, ancient in origin but rendered in colorful contemporary fabrics, will inspire, excite, and delight you. As you choose a crest design for your quilt, first leaf through the pages of *Circles of the East*. Enjoy the photographs and read the fascinating stories. This should help inspire you.

Where to Begin

If you have made quilts from Kumiko Sudo's earlier books, *East Quilts West*, *East Quilts West II*, or *Fabled Flowers*, you will already be familiar with the format of this book. If you are new to Kumiko's work, you will immediately notice that *Circles of the East* is not like other quilting books. The designs, the colors, the fabrics all come together in a unique blending of Eastern and Western cultures. As you are reading, why not try to create an atmosphere that will help you understand a little more about Kumiko's cultural heritage? Play some Japanese music in the background. Sip a cup of green tea. Read the stories that tell you about each of the crest designs before you decide which ones to make. All of these suggestions can help you feel at ease and enter into the spirit of Kumiko's quilts.

In the past, Kumiko used silk from old Japanese garments to make quilts. In this book, she uses contemporary American fabrics. Yet in many cases, the overall effect still reflects a

20

Japanese sensibility. Since the fabrics are available in the United States, you can probably duplicate Kumiko's choices.

However, Kumiko feels that color is an individual expression, and her selections are intended for inspiration, not for instruction. In Japan, certain colors and design patterns have symbolic meaning. This is just one way in which Kumiko's cultural heritage has influenced her work, giving her quilts their unique character. You can use *Circles of the East* to make a "Kumiko quilt," or you can use your own color and fabric combinations to create one that has your own individual imprint on it.

Pointers on Technique

Circles of the East differs from other quilting books not only in design and spirit, but in technical matters, too. To ensure successful and enjoyable quilt making, keep these points in mind.

- *Circles of the East* is intended for people who have at least basic skills in sewing and quilt making, as well as for talented beginners.

- Experienced quilters should find the thirty block designs easy to make. Six of the designs also include instructions and fabric requirements for making full quilts. Beginners should start with one of these to familiarize themselves with Kumiko's methods of sewing and assembly. Then you can go on to make other blocks more easily, comfortably, and confidently.

- All of the crest designs involve sewing curved seams. For perfect curved seams, Kumiko prefers to use a form of appliqué. Her technique involves placing a fabric piece, with the seam allowance folded under, on top of the background square; the piece is then blind-stitched by hand. Kumiko stitches everything—curved and straight—by hand. Although the results are excellent when sewn by machine, Kumiko prefers to sew by hand, as she feels that, "the hand is directed not only by the eye but by the heart." The machine puts a distance between her and her work.

- The fabric charts may seem to specify an overly generous amount of fabric in some cases. This is because curved pieces take up more space and result in more wasted fabric than straight-line templates. In addition, it is far better to have a bit too much fabric than too little.

- The fabric requirements for borders on the quilts are figured without piecing if they are over 2" (5 cm) wide. Narrower borders are figured to be pieced, to save fabric. Of course, the decision to piece or not to piece is up to you. Sometimes the border is of one of the fabrics that appear in the block; in this case, you may want to use the waste fabric from the border to make the block pieces.

- Full-size templates for all blocks are provided at the back of the book. All measurements include a ¼" (0.8 cm) seam allowance, unless otherwise indicated. All templates require adding a ¼" (0.8 cm) seam allowance, unless otherwise indicated. Small template pieces require less than ¼" (0.8 cm) seam allowance.

- Instructions are given for making block and quilt tops only. To finish your project, you will need to buy batting and backing fabric, assemble the layers, and quilt them together. Kumiko considers quilting to be an accent, "rather than something to be seen all over the picture." In quilts used as wall hangings such accent stitching will suffice; however, quilts used as bedding will require more extensive quilting. Kumiko seldom draws a design, but usually quilts freestyle. She rarely uses thread to match the fabric—for example, she often uses purple thread for yellow fabric, and green for blue fabric—and may use two or three different thread colors in one quilt.

- Experiment. Use your imagination. You may want to make a whole quilt or make several individual blocks in different designs. The generous block size makes them ideal for small wall hangings, pillows, or other projects. You can also add to or subtract from the width and number of borders to get a variety of effects and a variety of sizes.

Creating New Kamon Quilts

Once you have made some of the blocks and the full quilts in *Circles of the East*, it is time to use *kamon* to create new designs of your own. You will notice as you look at the instructions for making five of the full quilts—*Plum Blossom*, *Chrysanthemum Variation*, *Wild Mandarin*, *Lily*, and *Nandina*—that Kumiko has rearranged the templates to create an overall quilt design that is pleasing to her. Sometimes, she has added new template pieces or varied the sizes of template pieces to further enrich her designs. *Chrysanthemum Variation*, *Wild Mandarin*, and *Nandina* are examples. The secret is to arrange and rearrange the templates, varying the size of the pieces as necessary, to create an overall design that delights you. The same is true of your color choices. Try not to stick rigidly to the fabrics you first select for a quilt. Go to your fabric stash and pull together colors that you do not always use and that, at first, may even be unappealing to you. You will be surprised how combining an unusual color with one of your favorite fabrics can make a quilt come to life.

To create your own series of *kamon* quilts, why not go back to the original *kamon* designs to find crests that are not included in *Circles of the East*? The best English-language reference is *The Elements of Japanese Design*, by John W. Dower, listed in the Bibliography. More than 2,700 crests are illustrated from which you can choose.

Blocks and Quilts

Peony

In the Japanese flower calendar, the month of June is represented by the peony. This lovely flower symbolizes joyous life and prosperity, happy marriage and virility. The peony was one of the most favored flowers of the early court nobility. First used for purely decorative purposes, it evolved as a very prestigious family crest. As the emblem of two of Japan's most aristocratic families, the peony crest was sought by feudal lords who hoped to impress others with their financial and political powers and their military connections. It was also chosen as the emblem of several influential temples and shrines. There are at least thirty different variations of the peony crest. I chose one that consists of a single large flower and two leaves, big and small, that are arranged to form a boundless circle.

TO MAKE THE CREST

First cut the number of pieces indicated on the templates on pages 76 to 77. Sew the pieces together in the following sequence, using the diagram as a guide.

1. Cut a base square of background fabric measuring 14½" × 14½" (37 cm × 37 cm).
2. Lay out all of the templates on the base square and draw guide lines.
3. Appliqué leaf J onto the base fabric, followed by stem pieces K and L.
4. Appliqué stem piece O, and P on top of O.
5. Appliqué piece N.
6. Appliqué the petals in the following order: A, B, C, D, E, F, G, H, and I.
7. Appliqué piece M.

Finished block size: 14" × 14" (36 cm × 36 cm)

26

Cherry Blossoms on a Tanzaku

Among the Heian nobility, the writing of poetry was an essential element of cultured life. A tanzaku is a narrow strip of rice paper, perfect for a waka, which is a classic Japanese poem form with thirty-one letters arranged in lines of five, seven, five, seven, and seven characters per line. It was surely practiced by the Heian nobility. The cherry blossom has, since the tenth century, been the favorite flower of Japan. It is no doubt so popular because, unlike many other flowers that had been imported from China, the cherry tree is native to Japan. It was originally found wild in the foothills around Nara and Kyoto, but eventually came to be cultivated in the formal gardens of Kyoto. Annual spring viewings of the blossoms were a regular ritual of the noble society of the Heian period. Surely this crest was designed by a Heian poet who found himself at a viewing of cherry trees, with his paper and brush happily at hand.

To Make the Crest

First cut the number of pieces indicated on the templates on pages 78 to 79. Sew the pieces together in the following sequence, using the diagram as a guide.

1. Cut a base square of background fabric measuring 14½" × 14½" (37 cm × 37 cm).
2. Lay out all of the templates on the base square and draw guide lines.
3. On the base fabric, appliqué piece A.
4. Appliqué B-1 and B-2 pieces.
5. Appliqué C, D, E, F, and G ribbon pieces in that order.
6. Appliqué two H pieces onto piece G.
7. Appliqué four U bud pieces.
8. Appliqué two R, one S, and one T pieces.
9. Appliqué two K, one L, two V, and one W pieces.
10. Appliqué leaves Q, P, and N at the bottom right.
11. Appliqué three M cherry blossoms.
12. Appliqué Tanzaku pieces I and J.
13. Appliqué leaves N, O, and P.

Finished block size: 14" × 14" (36 cm × 36 cm)

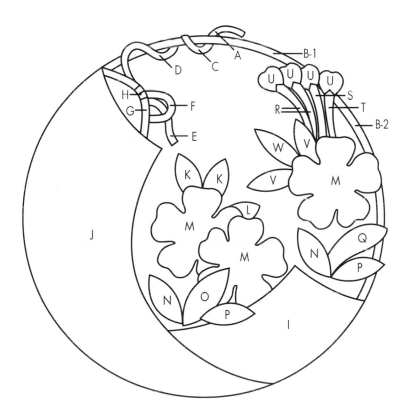

27

Wood Sorrel

The wood sorrel is a weed noted for its ability to reproduce itself. In Japan it enjoyed a broad popularity and was sought as a crest by warriors. The virility of the perennial plant was seen as a good-luck charm for the prosperity of their families. The blossom of the plant is a delicate five-petaled affair, but it is the three-lobed leaf, similar to a clover, that is the subject of the twenty-five or so different crests of the wood sorrel design. In the design shown here, look for the sword blades around the red flower at the center. The practice of adding a martial flavor to a traditional crest came about as the samurai class began using family crests. Wood sorrel was used as a medicinal herb in the early days of Japan. It was also called "mirror plant" because its leaves were used to polish bronze mirrors; its design is sometimes found etched into the backs of such mirrors.

TO MAKE THE CREST

First cut the number of pieces indicated on the templates on page 80. Sew the pieces together in the following sequence, using the diagram as a guide.

1. Cut a base square of background fabric measuring 14½" × 14½" (37 cm × 37 cm).
2. Lay out all of the templates on the base square and draw guide lines.
3. Draw a 9¾" (24.8 cm) circle for a guide line onto the base fabric.
4. Appliqué one E piece and one E-R along the circle line. Repeat twice.
5. Appliqué the petal pieces F, G, H, and I in alphabetical order, with J in the center. Repeat twice.
6. Appliqué three A pieces in the center of the circle.
7. Appliqué three B pieces in between.
8. Appliqué piece C in the center of pieces A and B.

Finished block size: 14" × 14" (36 cm × 36 cm)

Flower Diamond

The diamond is an ancient symbol, brought into Japan from China before the Heian period, and was a favorite in textile design even before the custom of family crests was adopted. It was believed to be an amulet that guarded the four corners of a home. The diamond shaped leaves of the water chestnut are thought to be the source from which the Japanese word for diamond, hishi, is taken. Many warriors liked this shape and used the hishi design on their armor. One of the earliest known Japanese textile patterns was the "flower diamond," which interpreted a four-petaled flower into a diamond shape. In this design, the hishi was adapted to form a butterfly. You can see how each petal of the original four-petaled flower diamond has been manipulated to make the butterfly shape: first, the two opposite petals were lengthened, then shaped to make the wings; next, the remaining two petals were manipulated to make the body of the butterfly.

TO MAKE THE CREST

First cut the number of pieces indicated on the templates on page 81. Sew the pieces together in the following sequence, using the diagram as a guide.

1. Cut a base square of background fabric measuring 14½" × 14½" (37 cm × 37 cm).
2. Lay out all of the templates on the base square and draw guide lines.
3. Baste one A piece, two B pieces, and one C piece onto the base fabric. Repeat twice.
4. Appliqué one F, one F-R piece, one D piece, and one E piece over the pieces that are basted in place onto No. 3. Repeat twice.
5. Appliqué one G piece and one G-R piece onto the base fabric. Appliqué piece H in the center. Repeat twice.

Finished block size: 14" × 14" (36 cm × 36 cm)

Gingko

In the fall, the avenues of Tokyo are lined with golden gingko trees; their glittering leaves falling in the sunset is an unforgettable sight. Gingko, along with the oak and the crytomeria, were held in special veneration in the Shinto faith; they were revered as guardian trees because of the great size they could reach. Because a gingko tree bears thousands of nuts, its design in a family crest symbolizes prosperity for future generations. The nut itself is not used in crest designs, although it is edible and considered a delicacy in Japan. The leaf of the tree is the basis for the fifteen or so different crest designs based on the gingko. It is a rather unusual three-lobed leaf, in a simple fan shape that has been the same for thousands of years. Most crest designs use three leaves, like the one I have prepared for you.

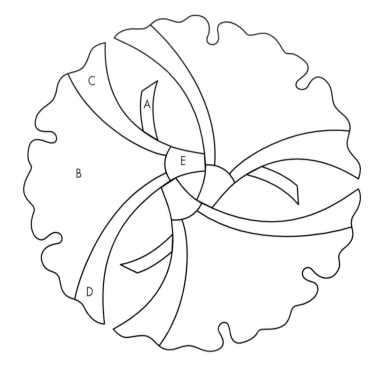

TO MAKE THE CREST

First cut the number of pieces indicated on the templates on page 82. Sew the pieces together in the following sequence, using the diagram as a guide.

1. Cut a base square of background fabric measuring 14½" × 14½" (37 cm × 37 cm).
2. Lay out all of the templates on the base square and draw guide lines.
3. Appliqué three A pieces onto the base fabric.
4. Appliqué three B pieces.
5. Appliqué three C pieces.
6. Appliqué three D pieces.
7. Appliqué three E pieces.

Finished block size: 14" × 14" (36 cm × 36 cm)

Gingko Quilt

Quilt size	39" × 43" (99 cm × 117 cm)	
Block size	14" × 14" (36 cm × 36 cm)	
Setting	2 × 2	
Blocks	4	

FABRIC AMOUNTS	YARDS	CM
Background blocks	½	46
Template A	⅛	11
Template B	¼	23
Template C	⅛	11
Template D	⅛	11
Template E	⅛	11
Sashing: 3" (7.6 cm)	¼	23
Center square	⅛	11
Top/bottom border: 6" (15.2 cm)	¼	23
Side border: 4" (10.2 cm)	¼	23

CUTTING	QUANTITY
Background squares: 14½" (37 cm)	4
Template A	12
Template B	12
Template C	12
Template D	12
Template E	12
Sashing: 3½" × 14½" (8.9 cm × 36.8 cm)	4
Center square: 3½" (8.9 cm)	1
Top/bottom border:	
6½" × 31½" (16.5 cm × 80 cm)	2
Side border:	
4½" × 43½" (11.4 cm × 110.5 cm)	2

To Make the Quilt

1. Cut four base squares of background fabric measuring 14½" × 14½" (37 cm × 37 cm).
2. Lay out all of the templates on the base squares and draw guide lines.
3. Make four blocks according to the directions on page 30.
4. Sew the sashing strips to the blocks and the center squares to the sashing strips as shown.
5. Attach the top and bottom borders.
6. Attach the side borders.

Butterfly Wheel

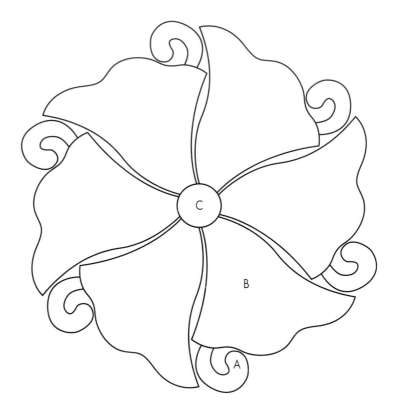

Some of the thousands of different family crests demonstrated a remarkable skill on the part of the designer at combining a pair of motifs, each with a particular significance, into a harmonious, breathtakingly beautiful whole. No better example exists than the butterfly wheel, an ingenious combination of two beloved themes. The butterfly is a very popular motif, and many crests simply feature its beautiful prismatic wings, in designs similar to this one. The butterfly in flight signifies pride of place, the warrior's close attachment to his native soil. The wheel, a Buddhist sacred symbol, has meaning of its own. It represents the teachings of Buddha, turning freely and crushing all obstacles in the mind. The samurai seem to have chosen it as a symbol to solicit divine assistance as they rolled over their enemies. This butterfly wheel speaks to both the warrior's pride of place and dominance over his enemies.

TO MAKE THE CREST

First cut the number of pieces indicated on the templates on page 83. Sew the pieces together in the following sequence, using the diagram as a guide.

1. Cut a base square of background fabric measuring 14½" × 14½" (37 cm × 37 cm).
2. Lay out all of the templates on the base square and draw guide lines.
3. Appliqué six A pieces onto the base.
4. Appliqué six B pieces, with one C piece in the center.

Finished block size: 14" × 14" (36 cm × 36 cm)

34

Maple

Red autumn leaves are simply beautiful, whether in the East or the West. Maple trees, especially, dye the woods and hills with their burning red color, explaining perhaps the choice of the maple as the flower of October. Special gatherings were held during the Heian Era to view the autumn foliage, during which the nobles held branches of red maple leaves over their shoulders. The tradition of holding these autumn festivities under the red maple trees has continued along with spring cherry blossom festivals. Although the maple is mentioned often in literature and was a decorative pattern for textiles very early in Japanese history, it is not one of the more popular motifs for family crests, a surprising distinction it shares with the cherry blossom. There are about ten different variations of the maple crest; I chose one that would allow me to express with color the maple trees gradually getting redder.

TO MAKE THE CREST

First cut the number of pieces indicated on the templates on pages 83 to 85. Sew the pieces together in the following sequence, using the diagram as a guide.

1. Cut a base square of background fabric measuring 14½" × 14½" (37 cm × 37 cm).
2. Lay out all of the templates on the base square and draw guide lines.
3. Appliqué the stem pieces A, B, C, D, E, F, and G.
4. Appliqué the outside stem pieces H-1, H-2, H-3, and I.
5. Appliqué the leaf pieces in order: J, K, L, M, N, O, P, Q, and R.

Finished block size: 14" × 14" (36 cm × 36 cm)

Wisteria Variation

In Japanese, the word for wisteria is fuji. It comes as no surprise, then, that it was part of the family crest of the Fujiwara family, whose name literally means "field of wisteria." The Fujiwara were known all over the country as a brave Bushi (samurai) family in the northeastern part of Japan during the Heian period. Almost all of the other families whose last names had the character "fuji" used the wisteria flower for their family crests. Therefore, there are hundreds of variations in wisteria family crests. The people in Japan enjoy banquets under wisteria flowers in early summer. Its beautiful color and shape have caught the hearts of the people. The wisteria motif has been a popular choice in women's kimono design. This particular wisteria family crest is called Rikyu-fuji. It may have come from the name of the famous founder of the tea ceremony, Senno Rikyu, who was a ruler during the civil wars. He must have loved the flower.

TO MAKE THE CREST

First cut the number of pieces indicated on the templates on page 86. Sew the pieces together in the following sequence, using the diagram as a guide.

1. Cut a base square of background fabric measuring 14½" × 14½" (37 cm × 37 cm).
2. Lay out all of the templates on the base square and draw guide lines.
3. Appliqué A-A, A-B, and A-C onto the base fabric. Reverse the three pieces and repeat.
4. Appliqué B, then C onto B. Reverse these pieces and repeat.
5. Appliqué four D pieces.
6. Appliqué E and F pieces. Reverse these pieces and repeat.
7. Baste three H pieces onto the center of the base fabric.
8. Appliqué three G pieces over the pieces that are basted in place onto No. 7.
9. Appliqué I onto No. 8, in the center of the circle.

Finished block size: 14" × 14" (36 cm × 36 cm)

Feather Duster

The feather duster may seem an odd choice as a crest for a social class who did not do their own dusting, and indeed it is a very rare family crest design. However, when its association with the tea ceremony is explained, the choice becomes more understandable. A duster of white hawk feathers, symbolizing the sacred bird of Chinese legend, would have been used to cleanse the tea room at the beginning of the ceremony. Next, a bird feather duster was employed to remove any dust from tea ceremony utensils. The designer of this crest undertook to symbolize a bird flying to the sky, testing the limits of exhaustion. It may also be thought to represent the two types of dusters used in the tea ceremony. I arranged the colors carefully to emphasize the uniqueness of this design.

To Make the Crest

First cut the number of pieces indicated on the templates on pages 87 to 88. Sew the pieces together in the following sequence, using the diagram as a guide.

1. Cut a base square of background fabric measuring 14½" × 14½" (37 cm × 37 cm).
2. Lay out all of the templates on the base square and draw guide lines.
3. Appliqué one A piece onto the base fabric. Reverse this piece and repeat for the other side.
4. Appliqué feather pieces B, C, D, E, F, and G onto the base fabric in alphabetical order. Reverse these pieces and repeat on the other side.
5. Appliqué H, I, and J onto No. 4. Reverse the pieces and repeat on the other side.
6. Appliqué piece K onto No. 5. Reverse it and repeat on the other side.
7. Appliqué L, M, N, and O onto No. 6. Reverse and repeat on other side.
8. Appliqué piece P onto No. 7. Reverse and repeat on other side.
9. Appliqué piece Q onto No. 8.
10. Appliqué piece R onto No. 9.

Finished block size: 14" × 14" (36 cm × 36 cm)

Plum Blossom

The plum tree was introduced to Japan about 1,200 years ago for use in medicines and dyes. Later it became popular as an ornamental garden flower because of its loveliness and pleasant fragrance. Michizane Sugawara, a famous ninth-century poet, loved the plum. He was venerated after his death as Tenjin-sama, the patron god of learning, poetry, and calligraphy. The shrine to Tenjin adopted the plum blossom as its official crest, and in later years, Japanese families chose the plum blossom to indicate that they were either of the lineage of Michizane or worshippers at the shrine. The plum blossom was a traditional symbol of fortitude in all the Orient, for it braves the lingering chill of winter to bloom before all other flowers. With the pine and bamboo, it is one of the "three companions of the deep cold." It is the flower of February. This lovely crest design, of plum blossoms on a packet of incense, appeals to me because of the wonderful possibilities for use of color.

To Make the Crest

First cut the number of pieces indicated on the templates on pages 88 to 90. Sew the pieces together in the following sequence, using the diagram as a guide.

1. Cut a base square of background fabric measuring 14½" × 14½" (37 cm × 37 cm).
2. Lay out all of the templates on the base square and draw guide lines.
3. Appliqué piece A onto the base fabric, and then appliqué B onto A.
4. Appliqué piece C, then two D pieces over C. Appliqué E, F, and G, in that order.
5. Sew piece H and piece J to piece I, and appliqué this onto the base fabric.
6. Appliqué piece K to No. 5 and piece L onto K.
7. Appliqué pieces M, N, O, N, N, P, N, and N, onto No. 6, working from the top down.
8. Appliqué piece Q onto piece I, then two R pieces, then pieces S, T, and U.
9. Embroider five stamens on C and Q, using an outline stitch and French knot.

Finished block size: 14" × 14" (36 cm × 36 cm)

Plum Blossom Quilt

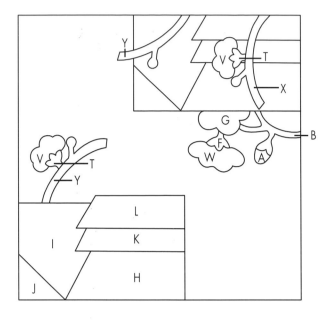

Quilt size	32" × 32" (81 cm × 81 cm)
Block size	14" × 14" (36 cm × 36 cm)
Setting	2 × 2
Blocks	4

FABRIC AMOUNTS	YARDS	CM
Background squares	1	91
Template A	⅛	11
Template B	⅛	11
Template F	⅛	11
Template G	⅛	11
Template H	¼	23
Template I	¼	23
Template J	¼	23
Template K	¼	23
Template L	¼	23
Template T	⅛	11
Template V	¼	23
Template W	⅛	11
Template X	⅛	11
Template Y	⅛	11
Border: 2" (5 cm)	¾	69

CUTTING	QUANTITY
Background squares: 14½" (37 cm)	4
Template A	4
Template B	4
Template F	4
Template G	4
Template H	8
Template I	8
Template J	8
Template K	8
Template L	8
Template T	8
Template V	8
Template W	4
Template X	4
Template Y	8
Border: 2½" × 30½" (6 cm × 77 cm)	4

To Make the Quilt

1. Cut four base squares of background fabric measuring 14½" × 14½" (37 cm × 37 cm).
2. Lay out all of the templates on the base squares and draw guide lines.
3. Sew piece J to piece I.
4. Sew piece L, K, and H to No. 3. Make two units for each block.
5. Appliqué pieces A, B, W, F, and G onto the background fabric.
6. Appliqué pieces V, T, and Y in that order onto the background fabric.
7. Appliqué the No. 4 units onto the background fabric.
8. Appliqué piece Y. Then appliqué pieces T and X onto the upper rectangle unit, as shown, then trim the block. Make four blocks total.
9. Sew the blocks together, as shown.
10. Attach the borders, as shown.

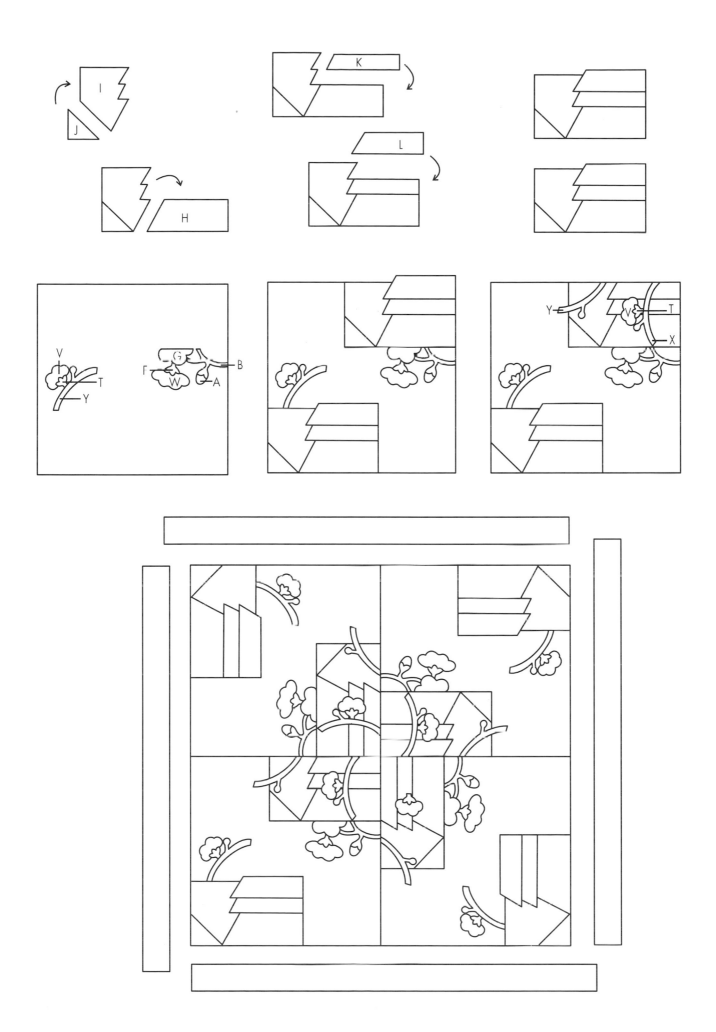

Pigeons in Mistletoe

The pigeon has, since ancient times, been considered divine, a guardian of shrines, and the messenger of Hachiman, god of war. After a battle, the winning side would release pigeons, and images of pigeons were drawn onto battleflags after a reconciliation. Mistletoe was much admired in court society of eastern Japan, where the elite of the samurai class lived. Because Hachiman was the patron saint of battle and mistletoe was a favorite plant of warriors, mistletoe became associated with Hachiman. Since it lives on after other plants have succumbed to winter, mistletoe is also a symbol of prosperity. A legend surrounds the pigeon-and-mistletoe crest. During a battle in which he was forced to flee, Yoritomo hid in a hollow tree. As enemy scouts combed the area, one ran his sword into the tree, touching Yoritomo's sleeve. Yoritomo prayed fervently to Hachiman that he be spared. At that moment, two pigeons, Hachiman's messengers, flew noisily out of the hole in the tree, diverting the attention of the searchers.

To Make the Crest

First cut the number of pieces indicated on the templates on page 91. Sew the pieces together in the following sequence, using the diagram as a guide.

1. Cut a base square of background fabric measuring 14½" × 14½" (37 cm × 37 cm).
2. Lay out all of the templates on the base square and draw guide lines.
3. Appliqué leaf pieces A, B, C, D, and E in alphabetical order onto the base fabric. Reverse these pieces and repeat for other side.
4. Appliqué pieces F, G, and H for the pigeon onto the leaves. Reverse these pieces and repeat for other side.

Finished block size: 14" × 14" (36 cm × 36 cm)

42

Gentian

Perhaps because its purple–blue flowers appear in the fall, the gentian has traditionally represented autumnal loneliness in Japanese literature. However, as a crest, it is a good example of the type of design that was used for purely decorative purposes, adapted for its charming beauty. It was popular among the aristocracy during the Heian period, but it was not widely adapted by the warrior class. The roots of the gentian were treasured for their use as a stomach medicine. Variations of the gentian design, which number about twenty, can become quite elaborate. The one I chose for you is one of the simpler styles: it contains only two flowers, of different sizes, and one bud. Some of the designs incorporate as many as nine flowers, in different sizes, with masses of leaves. I choose purple to represent the clothing of the Heian nobles and blue for the autumn sky. The beautiful star that appears at the center of each flower is done in gold.

To Make the Crest

First cut the number of pieces indicated on the templates on pages 92 to 93. Sew the pieces together in the following sequence, using the diagram as a guide.

1. Cut a base square of background fabric measuring 14½" × 14½" (37 cm × 37 cm).
2. Lay out all of the templates on the base square and draw guide lines.
3. Appliqué piece A onto the base fabric. Appliqué B, C, D, and E (in that order) onto the base fabric.
4. Appliqué pieces F and L, and then piece M onto L.
5. Appliqué leaf pieces N, K, O, and P (in that order).
6. Baste G to the base fabric. Appliqué I, I-R, J, J-R and one H piece over G.
7. Baste Q to the base fabric. Appliqué R, R-R, T, T-R and one S piece over Q.

Finished block size: 14" × 14" (36 cm × 36 cm)

Noshi

Noshi is the decoration added to a gift on special occasions like New Year's Day, weddings, or feast days. This tradition is at least five hundred years old. The original noshi was made of abalone, a shellfish. The meat was thinly sliced, stretched, and dried in the sun, then cut into thin strips and wrapped with rice paper. It has a pleasant scent and lasts almost forever, explaining perhaps why the tradition has survived. Today, noshi are made of folded paper. The word noshi *means "to expand"; in other words, to prosper. This fortuitous symbolism goes far to explaining its popularity as a crest design: more than twenty-five designs, with little or no common thread to unite them other than they are comprised of thin strips, have been gathered under the noshi name. I chose this crest because I admire the craftsmanship that creates from the noshi a delicate butterfly pattern. In this joyful image, the warm colors suggest a butterfly dancing in celebration.*

TO MAKE THE CREST

First cut the number of pieces indicated on the templates on pages 94 to 95. Sew the pieces together in the following sequence, using the diagram as a guide.

1. Cut a base square of background fabric measuring 14½" × 14½" (37 cm × 37 cm).
2. Lay out all of the templates on the base square and draw guide lines.
3. Appliqué the butterfly legs: four each of A and B pieces.
4. Appliqué the antenna piece C.
5. Appliqué the feather pieces in alphabetical order: D, E, F, G, H, I, and J.
6. Appliqué the feather pieces K, L, and M.
7. Appliqué two N pieces onto No. 6.

Finished block size: 14" × 14" (36 cm × 36 cm)

44

Chrysanthemum

When the chrysanthemum first entered Japan from China, it was called the flower of the sunbeam because of its resemblance to the sun. Emperor Gotoba, of the Kamakura Era, had the design worked into his robes, palanquins and carriages, and even engraved on his swords. A century later Emperor Godaigo gave certain loyal subjects the right to wear the chrysanthemum. While the motif was fairly freely used as a family emblem even outside the immediate Imperial Family, it remained the most coveted of crests well through the sixteenth century. The flower itself is still well-loved in Japan; you can find it in even the smallest garden. Thought to be the elixir of life, the petals are used in tea, salad, and wine. In this design, the combination of warm and cool colors attempts to capture the spirit of the chrysanthemum.

TO MAKE THE CREST

First cut the number of pieces indicated on the templates on pages 96 to 98. Sew the pieces together in the following sequence, using the diagram as a guide.

1. Cut a base square of background fabric measuring 14½" × 14 ½" (37 cm × 37 cm).
2. Lay out all of the templates on the base square and draw guide lines.
3. Appliqué piece A onto the base fabric, and then appliqué piece B onto piece A.
4. Appliqué piece C onto the base fabric, and then appliqué pieces D and E onto piece C.
5. Appliqué piece F onto the base fabric, and then appliqué piece G onto piece F.
6. Appliqué piece H onto the base fabric, and then appliqué pieces I, J, K, and L.
7. Appliqué piece M onto the base fabric, and then appliqué piece N onto piece M.
8. Appliqué piece O onto the base fabric, and then appliqué piece P onto O. Appliqué Q, then R onto piece Q. Appliqué piece S, and then T onto piece S.
9. Appliqué piece U in the center of the flower.

Finished block size: 14" × 14" (36 cm × 36 cm)

45

Chrysanthemum Variation

There is a Chinese folk tale that tells of a group of mountain hermits who ate nothing but the crysanthemum and in that way lived to be ancient. And so, this flower is thought to be a symbol of long life. Another tale tells of a mountain village so overgrown with chrysanthemums that the blossoms floated in the mountain streams, and villagers who drank their waters rarely died before they reached one hundred years of age. Chrysanthemums, in their hundreds of different varieties, were a classic ornamental garden flower among the nobility from the Heian Era, and chrysanthemum-viewing parties graced the autumn lives of this courtly class. Each September, a chrysanthemum festival still takes place, featuring flower shows and a special chrysanthemum wine. The crest I have chosen shows an interesting reverse view of chrysanthemum blossoms. This was a trick employed by the ancient Japanese draftsmen who labored to make new variations of this popular motif.

TO MAKE THE CREST

First cut the number of pieces indicated on the templates on pages 99 to 100. Sew the pieces together in the following sequence, using the diagram as a guide.

1. Cut a base square of background fabric measuring 14½" × 14½" (37 cm × 37 cm).
2. Lay out all of the templates on the base square and draw guide lines.
3. Appliqué two B pieces to the base fabric.
4. Appliqué two C pieces to the base fabric.
5. Appliqué two D pieces to the base fabric.
6. Appliqué two A pieces to the base fabric.
7. Appliqué two each of pieces E, F, and G onto the base fabric, followed by one of H.
8. Appliqué piece I in the center of the design.

Finished block size: 14" × 14" (36 cm × 36 cm)

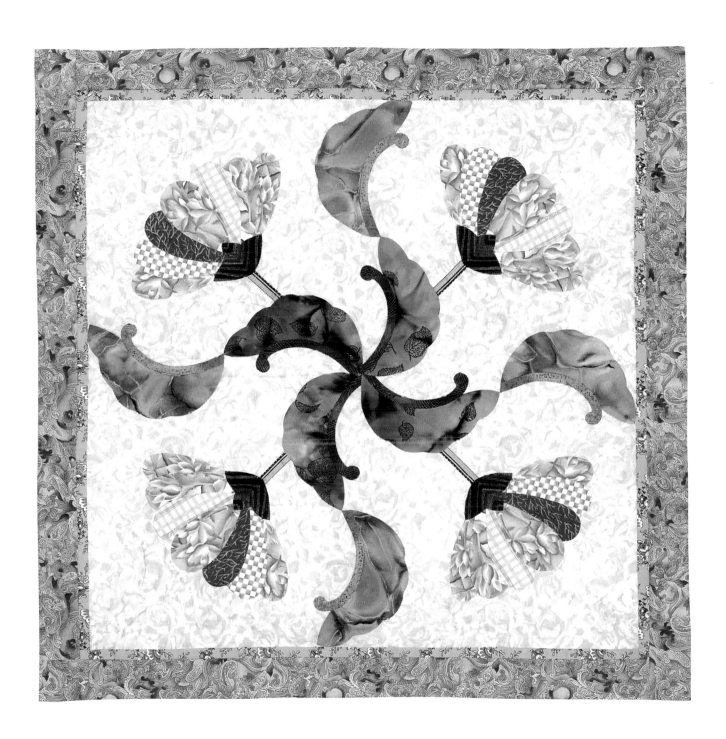

Chrysanthemum Variation Quilt

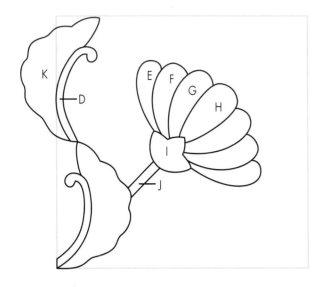

Quilt size	33" × 33" (84 cm × 84 cm)	
Block size	28" × 28" (72 cm × 72 cm)	
Block	1	

FABRIC AMOUNTS	YARDS	CM
Background blocks	1	91
Template D	¼	23
Template E	⅛	11
Template F	⅛	11
Template G	⅛	11
Template H	⅛	11
Template I	⅛	11
Template J	⅛	11
Template K	¼	23
Inside border: ¾" (2 cm)	⅛	11
Outside border: 2" (5 cm)	¼	23

CUTTING	QUANTITY
Background squares: 28½" (72.5 cm)	1
Template D	8 (Reverse 4)
Template E	8 (Reverse 4)
Template F	8 (Reverse 4)
Template G	8 (Reverse 4)
Template H	4
Template I	4
Template J	4
Template K	8 (Reverse 4)

Inside border:
  1¼" × 29¼" (3.5 cm × 74.5 cm)   4
Outside border:
  2½" × 32" (6.5 cm × 81.5 cm)   4

TO MAKE THE QUILT

1. Cut one base square of background fabric measuring 28½" × 28½" (72.4 cm × 72.4 cm).
2. Fold the background square into fourths to make creases, then lay out all of the templates and draw guide lines.
3. Sew pieces E, F, and G together.
4. Sew pieces E-R, F-R, and G-R together.
5. Sew No. 3 and No. 4 to piece H.
6. Sew pieces I and J together, then appliqué onto the flower shape.
7. Repeat Steps 3 to 6 to make four flowers
8. Appliqué the flower shapes onto the background fabric.
9. Sew piece K to D and piece K-R to D-R. Make four of each. Appliqué these units onto the background fabric.
10. Attach the inner and outer borders, as shown.

Genji Wheel

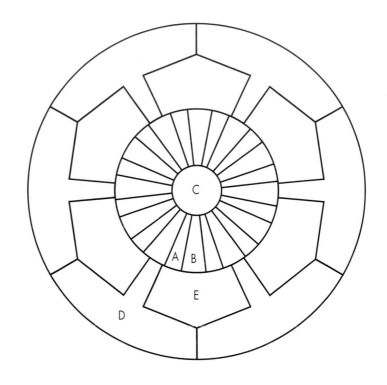

There are several origins of the wheel crest. In the earliest days, it was used to adorn garments and utensils. A thousand years ago, in the Heian Era, noble families built their own carts or carriages, elaborately decorated with gold and silver, Japanese lacquer, seashell art, and even detailed paintings. This embellishment was deemed necessary, since the nobles rode in their carts to ceremonies at court and at various shrines. Each would ascend into his magnificent cart, with its attached incense burner alight, and enjoy the ride, flipping his layered kimono sleeves in the wind. The large wheels of the carts provided a perfect palette for creative decoration. The wheel crest has been worn by devoted Buddhists for religious reasons. The wheel of the law is a Buddhist ritual object, shaped with blade-like spokes radiating from the hub. It is of varying forms, according to the number of spokes.

To Make the Crest

First cut the number of pieces indicated on the templates on page 101. Sew the pieces together in the following sequence, using the diagram as a guide.

1. Cut a base square of background fabric measuring 14½" × 14½" (37 cm × 37 cm).
2. Lay out all of the templates on the base square and draw guide lines.
3. Draw a 9" (23 cm) circle for a guide line on the base fabric.
4. Appliqué six D pieces along the guide line.
5. Appliqué one E piece between two D pieces (six in total).
6. Baste twelve A pieces onto the base.
7. Appliqué twelve B pieces onto No. 6.
8. Appliqué piece C in the center.

Finished block size: 14" × 14" (36 cm × 36 cm)

Camellia

The Japanese reverence for nature manifests itself in its decorative arts, in water color drawings, in kimono, and in pottery designs. Practically every flower and tree that grows in the country has been adapted as a motif for a family crest. Nobles had grand gardens and enjoyed seasonal floral displays—cherry blossoms in spring, iris, and wisterias in early summer, chrysanthemums and Japanese bush clovers in fall, and camellias and peonies in winter. There were special social gatherings just for viewing blossoms. A spring garden party was described as having a centerpiece of cherry blossom branches in a celadon porcelain vase, with the ladies gathered about in beautiful spring attire, making them look like flowers as well. Everything must have been in perfect harmony, with the colorful blossoms and the beauty of the kimono art complementing one another. For the Japanese, the camellia is a nostalgic flower. It is also quite dramatic, making this crest a strong design.

TO MAKE THE CREST

First cut the number of pieces indicated on the templates on page 101. Sew the pieces together in the following sequence, using the diagram as a guide.

1. Cut a base square of background fabric measuring 14½" ¥ 14½" (37 cm ¥ 37 cm).
2. Lay out all of the templates on the base square and draw guide lines.
3. Appliqué three F pieces, three H leaf pieces, and one I piece onto the center of the base fabric.
4. Appliqué the petal pieces A and B. Repeat twice.
5. Appliqué three C pistil pieces.
6. Appliqué pieces D, E, and G in that order. Repeat twice.

Finished block size: 14" ¥ 14" (36 cm ¥ 36 cm)

Sparrow in a Bamboo Cottage

In family crest design, the sparrow is very often paired with bamboo, a natural association because flocks of sparrows live in bamboo groves. The sparrow represents the virtue of repaying one's obligations, and bamboo represents the blessings of good friends visiting a happy home. It is difficult to overstate the importance of bamboo to the Japanese. It binds the soil against flood and earthquake, provides crisp food in its young shoots, and serves literally thousands of daily purposes, from scaffolding to musical instruments to furniture. Primitive people thought the blooming of bamboo forecast a disaster, because, depending on the species, bamboo blooms only every 30, 60, or even 120 years, and then it dies. And, all plants of the species die simultaneously wherever it is found in the world. All Japanese children read a fairy tale called *Sweet Home of Sparrows.* I can imagine the designer of this family crest, with a cup of green tea in his hand, watching sparrows flying around in a bamboo woods.

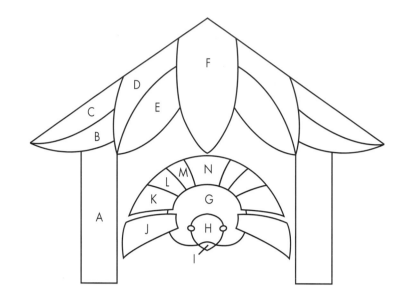

TO MAKE THE CREST

First cut the number of pieces indicated on the templates on page 102. Sew the pieces together in the following sequence, using the diagram as a guide.

1. Cut a base square of background fabric measuring 14½" ¥ 14½" (37 cm ¥ 37 cm).
2. Lay out all of the templates on the base square and draw guide lines.
3. Appliqué one A piece and one A-R onto the base fabric.
4. Appliqué B, B-R, C, C-R, D, D-R, E, E-R and F pieces of bamboo leaves onto the base fabric in alphabetical order.
5. Appliqué the sparrow in the middle of the fabric in this order: G, H, I, J, J-R, K, K-R, L, L-R, M, M-R, and N.
6. Embroider the eyes of the sparrow. (Or appliqué very tiny pieces of fabric for the eyes.)

Finished block size: 14" ¥ 14" (36 cm ¥ 36 cm)

Wisteria

Wisteria is the flower of April in Japan. It is found growing wild in the Kyoto-Osaka region, and as literary allusions make clear, it was already much admired in the Nara period. It was eventually domesticated and trained to grow on arbors and trellises in formal gardens. The first wisteria-viewing ceremonies were held during the reign of the Emperor Daigo (897-930). There are many wisteria family crests with their combinations of elegant flowers and leaves. This design has a modern touch by using vines to emphasize the beauty of the flower. When I saw the two vines from each side crossing over to make a circle, I imagined princesses of the Heian Era with a basketful of wisteria flowers. I arranged the design with bright, pretty colors for the images of the lovely princesses.

TO MAKE THE CREST

First cut the number of pieces indicated on the templates on page 103. Sew the pieces together in the following sequence, using the diagram as a guide.

1. Cut a base square of background fabric measuring 14½" ¥ 14½" (37 cm ¥ 37 cm).
2. Lay out all of the templates on the base square and draw guide lines.
3. Appliqué one A piece in the upper center of the base fabric. Appliqué one B piece to the left.
4. Appliqué one A-B piece in the upper right of the base fabric.
5. Appliqué one C piece and one C-R piece.
6. Appliqué one D and one D-R flower piece over each C piece.
7. Appliqué one E and one E-R bud piece.
8. Appliqué one F leaf piece in the center of the two E pieces.
9. Appliqué one stem piece H.
10. Appliqué one G and one G-R leaf piece on either side of stem H.

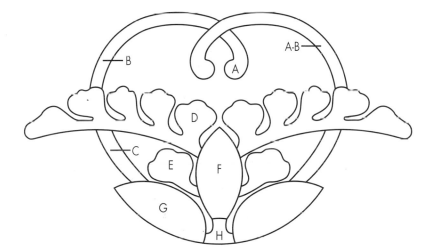

53

Wild Mandarin

The orange tree was brought to Japan from China in the third century A.D. and became an immediate favorite because of its glossy green leaves, sweet scent, and beautiful fruit. The five-petaled flowers, so sweet with scent in May, yield fruits in the fall. Orange trees, along with cherry trees, were traditionally planted at the front gates of palaces. Those trees are part of a display of Dolls of the Court that are a part of Girl's Day on March 3. Wild mandarin and cherry trees, made of fabric, flank the sides of each family's collection of formal dolls. Tachibana, or wild mandarin, is not quite the same as the orange tree—it bears tiny fruits that are not edible. Its white flowers give out the sweet scent of May. There are some twenty-five different crests that use the orange. In some very sophisticated designs, the blossom, leaf, and fruit are all depicted. I have chosen a triple diamond form, which was, I have to say, a real challenge to infuse with colors that pleased me.

TO MAKE THE CREST

First cut the number of pieces indicated on the templates on pages 105. Sew the pieces together in the following sequence, using the diagram as a guide.

1. Cut a base square of background fabric measuring 14½" ¥ 14½" (37 cm ¥ 37 cm).
2. Lay out all of the templates on the base square and draw guide lines.
3. Appliqué A, B, and C onto the base fabric, then A-R, B-R, and C-R.
4. Appliqué D, E, and F, then D-R, E-R, and F-R.
5. Appliqué two H pieces, one G piece, one I, one I-R, and one J piece in the order given.
6. Appliqué two L pieces, one K, one M, one M-R, and one N piece in the order given.
7. Appliqué two O pieces, one P, one Q, one Q-R, and one R piece in the order given.
8. Appliqué piece S last.

Finished block size: 14" ¥ 14" (36 cm ¥ 36 cm)

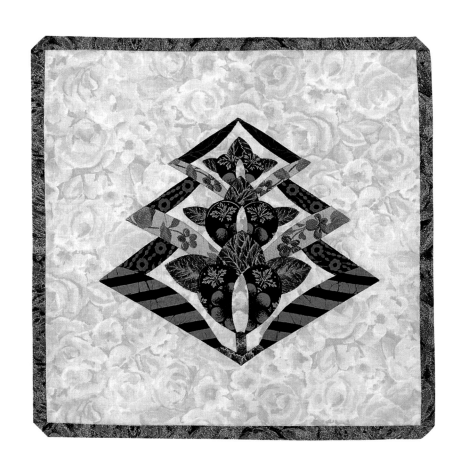

54

Wild Mandarin Quilt

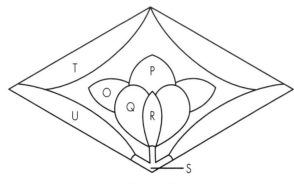

BLOCK A

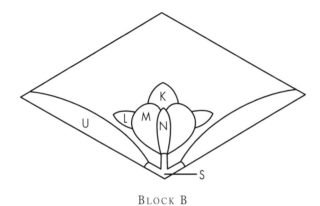

BLOCK B

TO MAKE THE QUILT

1. Cut sixteen diamond shaped base blocks of background fabric using the template on page 104.
2. Lay out all of the templates on the background pieces and draw guide lines.
3. For Block A, appliqué pieces O, P, and O-R onto the background fabric, in that order.
4. Appliqué pieces Q , Q-R, R, and S, in that order.
5. Appliqué pieces T and T-R along the top of the block. Appliqué pieces U and U-R along the bottom of the block, overlapping where necessary.
6. For Block B, appliqué pieces L, K, and L-R, in that order.
7. Appliqué pieces M, M-R, N, and S, in that order.
8. Appliqué pieces U and U-R along the bottom edge of the block.
9. Sew the blocks in rows, as shown.
10. Attach the inner and outer borders, as shown.

Diamond quilt size, each side	33" (84 cm)	
Diamond block size, each side	7" (18 cm)	
Setting	4 ¥ 4	
Block A	8	
Block B	8	

FABRIC AMOUNTS	YARDS	CM
Background diamonds		
(Mandrin Quilt Background)	1	91
Template K	⅛	11
Template L	⅛	11
Template M	⅛	11
Template N	⅛	11
Template O	⅛	11
Template P	⅛	11
Template Q	⅛	11
Template R	⅛	11
Template S	⅛	11
Template T	¼	23
Template U	½	46
Inside border: ½" (1.3 cm)	⅛	11
Outside border: 1¾" (4.4 cm)	⅛	11

CUTTING	QUANTITY
Background diamonds	
(Mandrin Quilt Background)	16
Template K	8
Template L	16 (Reverse 8)
Template M	16 (Reverse 8)
Template N	8
Template O	16 (Reverse 8)
Template P	8
Template Q	16 (Reverse 8)
Template R	8
Template S	16
Template T	16 (Reverse 8)
Template U	32 (Reverse 16)

Inside border:
1" ¥ 30" (1.3 cm ¥ 76 cm)	4

Outside border:
2¼" ¥ 33" (5.7 cm ¥ 83.8 cm)	4

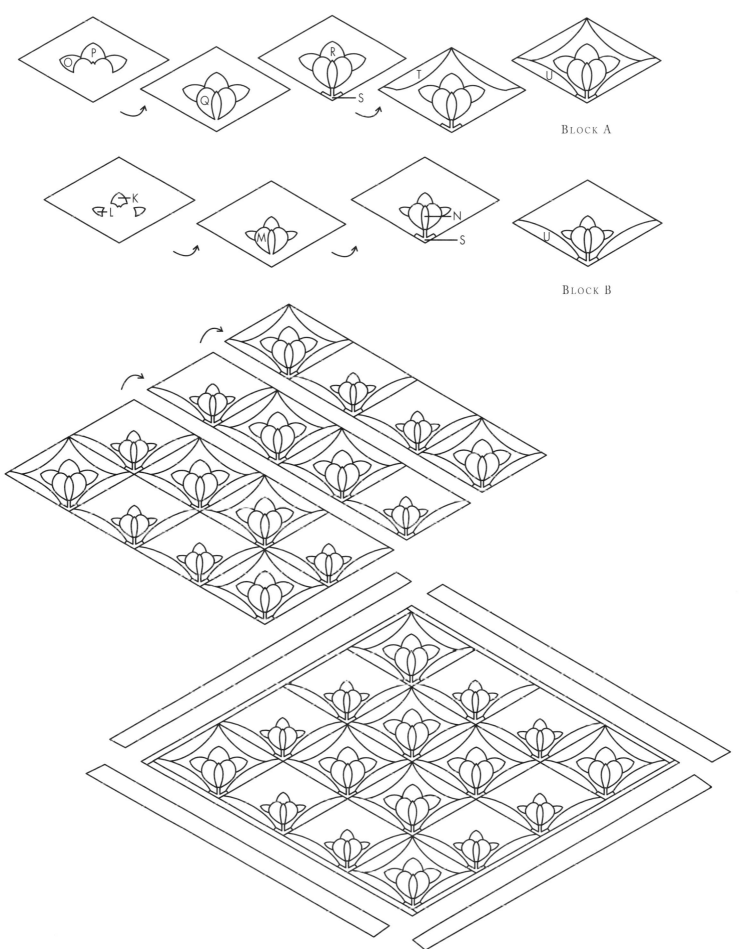

BLOCK A

BLOCK B

Mamezo Doll

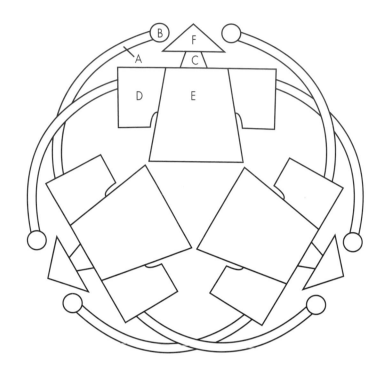

Mamezo was a homeless boy of the Genroku Era who made his living by street acrobatics. His achievements were such that eventually all street entertainers came to be called mamezo. By the mid-Edo period, his fame had led to the creation of a children's toy, a balancing doll made with beans and sticks. The word mamezo translates literally as "bean storehouse," a suitable name for the little doll. I imagine that the mamezo crest was probably used among the families of theater and playhouse owners, entertainers, and merchants. Of the five different crests that honor the mazemo doll, this is my favorite, because you can see the balancing poles that an acrobat uses, and these poles are so cleverly interwoven to form the traditional circle of all kamon. To honor the joy that Mamezo brought in his daily life, the laughter he created, I used an arrangement of bright, happy fabrics for the curved balances and his patched kimono.

TO MAKE THE CREST

First cut the number of pieces indicated on the templates on page 106. Sew the pieces together in the following sequence, using the diagram as a guide.

1. Cut a base square of background fabric measuring 14½" ¥ 14½" (37 cm ¥ 37 cm).
2. Lay out all of the templates on the base square and draw guide lines.
3. Appliqué piece A and then piece B onto A. Appliqué another piece A over the first A and then another B onto the A. Repeat twice.
4. Appliqué piece C and then piece F onto C.
5. Appliqué one D and one D-R piece.
6. Appliqué E onto No. 5.
7. Repeat Steps 4 to 6 twice.

Finished block size: 14" ¥ 14" (36 cm ¥ 36 cm)

Sailing Vessels

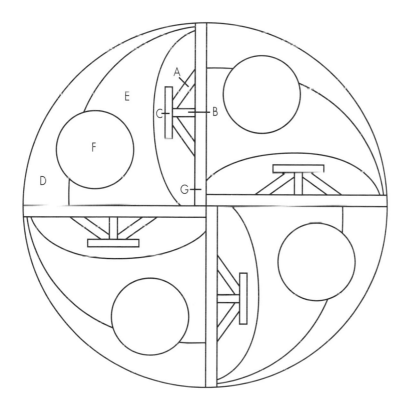

Not only did the sails of ships provide a wonderful backdrop on which to display a family crest in impressive size, they themselves provided inspiration for crest designs. However, for a country of islands, very little attention is given the sea in the development of Japanese heraldry. Most eyes seemed to be turned toward the land. The twenty-five designs that use sails or sailing vessels are as beautiful and graceful as any other, though not as widely adopted. The exception is the Nawa family, who, in 1333, successfully rescued the Emperor Godaigo from imprisonment on Oki Island by sailing him away from his captors. The emperor awarded the family a crest of sailing vessels. As a result, this majestic crest became a symbol of loyalty. The background of the four sailing vessels is covered with a material that expresses the raging waves of the Sea of Japan. It looks as if the sailing ships are running through the cold ocean on the wind.

TO MAKE THE CREST

First cut the number of pieces indicated on the templates on page 107. Sew the pieces together in the following sequence, using the diagram as a guide.

1. Cut a base square of background fabric measuring 14½" ¥ 14½" (37 cm ¥ 37 cm).
2. Lay out all of the templates on the base square and draw guide lines.
3. Draw a 10½" (25 cm) circle onto the base fabric.
4. Appliqué four D pieces around the edge of the circle, spacing them evenly.
5. Appliqué four E pieces onto the four D pieces.
6. Appliqué four F pieces onto No. 5.
7. Appliqué piece A and piece A-R onto the base fabric, then piece B and piece C. Repeat three times.
8. Appliqué four G pieces onto the base fabric.

Finished block size: 14" ¥ 14" (36 cm ¥ 36 cm)

Shinto Pendant

In medieval Japan, offerings of food, drink, or textiles were made to Shinto deities. In time, these were replaced by representative strips of paper folded into pendants. These were attached to staffs, which were laid on the altars of shrines. Eventually, the paper pendants came to represent the deities rather than the offerings. During the long and bloody civil wars, samurai dedicated paper pendants to purify themselves, attaching them to their horses, flags, or helmets. As the use of family crests emerged, many pendant designs were adopted; of the twenty-five or more variations, all show the staff as a long, slender rectangle, and all include the folded rice paper rectangles. Additional symbols sacred to the Shinto faith, such as gateways, bells, or mirrors, may be introduced to the crest design. The iron mirror represented in this crest is one of the three Imperial treasures of the Shinto religion. Lightning bolts are crafted of rice paper rectangles, and sacred evergreen branches flank each side of the design.

TO MAKE THE CREST

First cut the number of pieces indicated on the templates on page 108. Sew the pieces together in the following sequence, using the diagram as a guide.

1. Cut a base square of background fabric measuring 14½" ¥ 14½" (37 cm ¥ 37 cm).
2. Lay out all of the templates on the base square and draw guide lines.
3. Appliqué one A, one B, one B-R, and one A-R piece onto the base fabric in that order.
4. Appliqué piece C onto No. 3.
5. Appliqué piece D and piece D-R.
6. Appliqué E and F pieces.
7. Appliqué one G and one G-R pieces.
8. Appliqué four H leaves and three I leaves.
9. Appliqué piece J and piece J-R.
10. Appliqué four H-R and three I-R pieces.
11. Appliqué E-R and F-R pieces.
12. Appliqué three K pieces and three K-R pieces, overlapping from the bottom.
13. Appliqué L, and L-R pieces.
14. Appliqué piece M, and piece N onto M.

Finished block size: 14" ¥ 14" (36 cm ¥ 36 cm)

Butterfly

More than three hundred crest designs make use of the butterfly. Even before the period of Japanese heraldry, warriors frequently displayed this beloved image on their armor. Soldiers, when given the opportunity to select their first crest design, often chose the gentle butterfly. Even the bravest warriors, perhaps to demonstrate that their inner nature was different from their professional demeanor, made the butterfly their motif. Also, the Heian court nobles saw everlasting prosperity in a butterfly's transformation and flight into the great sky. Ancient though it is, this particular butterfly design has a very 1930s, art deco air about it. I chose to work with Japanese rice paper of the type used for origami, the art of paper folding, to execute this festive butterfly. Some crest designs are based on origami renderings of a particular subject; this motif could easily be an example.

TO MAKE THE CREST

First cut the number of pieces indicated on the templates on page 109. Sew the pieces together in the following sequence, using the diagram as a guide.

1. Cut a base square of background fabric measuring 14½" ¥ 14½" (37 cm ¥ 37 cm).
2. Lay out all of the templates on the base square and draw guide lines.
3. Appliqué A, A-R, B, B R, C, and C-R onto the base fabric.
4. Appliqué J, J-R, I, and I-R onto the base fabric.
5. Appliqué G and G-R. Then appliqué F and F-R.
6. Appliqué pieces D, D-R, E, E-R, H, H-R, K, K-R, and L, in that order.
7. Appliqué two M pieces and then an N piece onto No. 6.

Finished block size: 14" ¥ 14" (36 cm ¥ 36 cm)

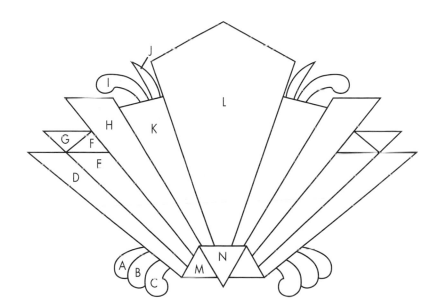

Lily

Lilies were not traditional design motifs in Japan. However, there are two types that have been found in family crests: the yuri, or ordinary (Asiatic) lily; and the hiogi, sometimes defined as the leopard flower or blackberry lily. Considering the beauty of the flower, it is surprising that no more than fifteen or so crests draw on the lily as a motif. It is possible that these designs came about during the time of the "floating world," when actors and courtesans alike were designing and wearing ever more beautiful and extravagant crests. Some of the crest designs are exquisitely literal representations of the flower, stalk, leaf, and bud; others are closeup views of single blossoms; still others include a supporting motif such as a bird or wave in the design. I have chosen to work with a design I call the "lily handball." In choosing colors for this design, I leaned toward the bold and adventurous.

TO MAKE THE CREST

First cut the number of pieces indicated on the templates on page 110. Sew the pieces together in the following sequence, using the diagram as a guide.

1. Cut a base square of background fabric measuring 14½" ¥ 14½" (37 cm ¥ 37 cm).
2. Lay out all of the templates on the base square and draw guide lines.
3. Appliqué petal pieces A, B, and C, in that order.
4. Appliqué pistil piece D onto No. 3.
5. Appliqué E and F.
6. Appliqué petals G and H onto No. 5.
7. Appliqué I and J.
8. Repeat Steps 3 to 7 twice.

Finished block size: 14" ¥ 14" (36 cm ¥ 36 cm)

Lily Quilt

TO MAKE THE QUILT

1. Cut eight base blocks of background fabric using the template on page 112.
2. Lay out all of the templates on the background pieces and draw guide lines.
3. Appliqué pieces A and B onto the background fabric and appliqué piece D onto B.
4. Appliqué pieces E and C, then pieces G and H.
5. Appliqué pieces I and J.
6. Sew the K and K-R triangles onto the corners of the background fabric.
7. Make four blocks and make four reversed blocks, for a total of eight blocks. Sew in rows of two together, as shown.
8. Sew the K and K-R triangles to the side sashing pieces and sew one sashing unit to both sides of each block row. Sew the rows together.
9. Sew the K and K-R triangles to the top and bottom sashing pieces. Sew two sashing units together and attach the outer border piece, as shown.
10. Sew the K and K-R triangles to the corner border pieces and attach to each side of No. 9.
11. Attach the top and bottom border pieces, then attach the side borders.

Quilt size	22" ¥ 49" (56 cm ¥ 124 cm)	
Block size	7½" ¥ 9½" (19.1 cm ¥ 24.1 cm)	
Setting	2 ¥ 4	
Blocks	8	

FABRIC AMOUNTS	YARDS	CM
Background blocks (Lily Quilt Background)	1	91
Template A	½	46
Template B	⅛	11
Template C	⅛	11
Template D	⅛	11
Template E	⅛	11
Template G	⅛	11
Template H	⅛	11
Template I	⅛	11
Template J	⅛	11
Template K	⅛	11
Side sashing	¼	23
Top/bottom sashing	¼	23
Side/corner border: 1½" (3.8 cm)	½	46
Top/bottom border: 2½" (6.4 cm)	⅛	23

CUTTING	QUANTITY
Background: (Lily Quilt Background)	8
Template A	8 (Reverse 4)
Template B	8 (Reverse 4)
Template C	8 (Reverse 4)
Template D	8 (Reverse 4)
Template E	8 (Reverse 4)
Template G	8 (Reverse 4)
Template H	8 (Reverse 4)
Template I	8 (Reverse 4)
Template J	8 (Reverse 4)
Template K	60 (Reverse 30)
Side sashing: Use template on page 111	8
Top/bottom sashing: Use template on page 111	4
Side border: 2" ¥ 38½" (5.1 cm ¥ 97.8 cm)	2
Corner border: Use template on page 111	4
Top/bottom border: 3" ¥ 15½" (7.6 cm ¥ 39.4 cm)	2

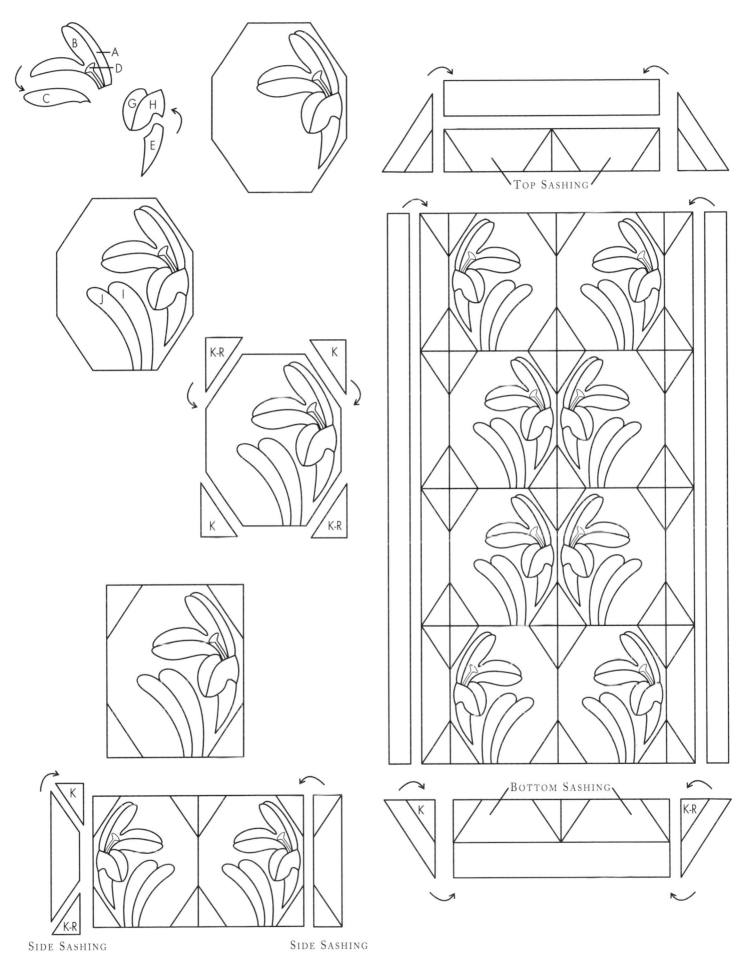

TOP SASHING

K-R   K

K   K-R

BOTTOM SASHING

K   K-R

K

K-R

SIDE SASHING   SIDE SASHING

B
A
D
C
G H
E

J I

65

Cherry Butterfly

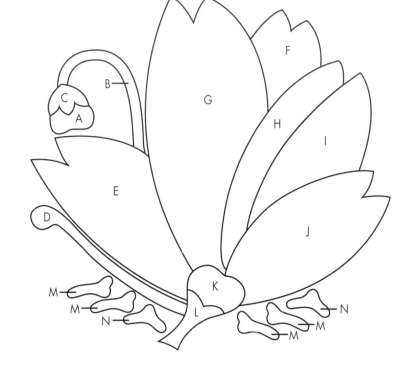

In spring many kinds of cherry trees burst into bloom all over the country, north to south, covering the mountainsides in glorious color. Paintings of the late Heian Era reveal the popularity of the cherry blossom as a pattern on clothing and utensils. A few noble families maintained it as a family crest. For example, the Yoshino family adopted the cherry blossom for their family symbol, because it immediately called to mind the springtime slopes of Mt. Yoshino. This design is typical of a convention brought to bear by ancient designers. One motif has been utilized in such a manner as to form another motif. A cherry blossom has been manipulated to form a butterfly shape, complete with antennae, feet, and proboscis. The two symbols of springtime are cleverly worked into a beautiful scene to inspire a storyteller or poet.

TO MAKE THE CREST

First cut the number of pieces indicated on the templates on pages 113 to 114. Sew the pieces together in the following sequence, using the diagram as a guide.

1. Cut a base square of background fabric measuring 14½" ¥ 14½" (37 cm ¥ 37 cm).
2. Lay out all of the templates on the base square and draw guide lines.
3. Appliqué pieces A, B, C, and D onto the base fabric in alphabetical order.
4. Appliqué pieces E, F, G, H, I, and J in alphabetical order.
5. Appliqué K and L onto No. 4.
6. Appliqué two M pieces, two M-R pieces, and two N pieces as indicated in the diagram.

Finished block size: 14" ¥ 14" (36 cm ¥ 36 cm)

66

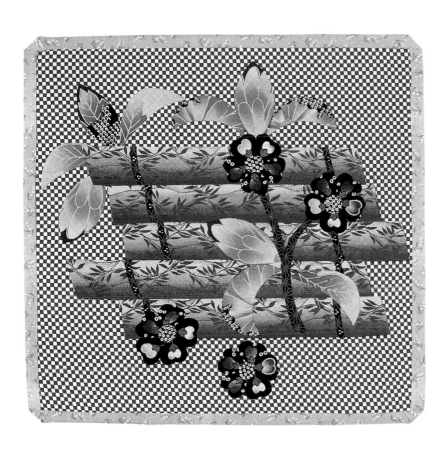

Raft

The nobility of old spent their days in pursuit of elegant pleasures. For example, on New Year's Day it was the custom to hold a gathering for the purpose of writing and enjoying poetry. One activity involved the group writing of a poem: one noble would begin the poem on a paper, then float it on a tiny raft down a garden brook, where another noble would pick it up and write another line, and so on until the poem was finished. Larger rafts were used as conveyances for pleasure outings on slow-moving rivers or streams. They were often decorated with flowers, especially cherry blossoms, and they, with their beautifully dressed passengers, presented a lovely sight to onlookers as they drifted downstream. This design shows a touch of the graceful spirit that filled ancient rafting activities. The bamboo raft is trimmed with cherry blossoms, a romantic touch for spring. The blue background fabric represents a peaceful brook.

TO MAKE THE CREST

First cut the number of pieces indicated on the templates on pages 115 to 117. Sew the pieces together in the following sequence, using the diagram as a guide.

1. Cut a base square of background fabric measuring 14½" ¥ 14½" (37 cm ¥ 37 cm).
2. Lay out all of the templates on the base square and draw guide lines.
3. In the left corner, appliqué leaf pieces A, B, C, and D.
4. Appliqué leaf pieces E, A, and E-R at the top on the right.
5. Appliqué raft pieces G, H, I, J, and K.
6. Appliqué nine L pieces onto the raft pieces as shown in the diagram.
7. Appliqué stem pieces M and N onto the raft pieces, followed by leaf pieces F, A, and D.
8. For each of the four flowers, appliqué five O petals in a circle with one P in the center. Place them as shown in the diagram.

Finished block size: 14" ¥ 14" (36 cm ¥ 36 cm)

Iris

The iris has been a metaphor for beauty from olden times because of its graceful shape and lovely fragrance. Its image was everywhere—on clothes, sliding doors, folding screens, boxes, storage chests. Its popularity endures today on such household items as porcelain. Perhaps the reason for its widespread popularity, other than its superb beauty, is that the iris was thought to be a protection against evil spirits. On the fifth day of the fifth month during the Heian Era, a great iris festival would be held; the belief was that at this time of the year the magic of the iris was most strong. The iris still represents May in the Japanese flower calendar. This crest is a gorgeous design that has a great iris on one half and thin leaves layered on the other half. I tried to convey the spectrum of these wonderful flowers of spring and early summer in this one iris.

TO MAKE THE CREST

First cut the number of pieces indicated on the templates on pages 117 to 119. Sew the pieces together in the following sequence, using the diagram as a guide.

1. Cut a base square of background fabric measuring 14½" ¥ 14½" (37 cm ¥ 37 cm).
2. Lay out all of the templates on the base square and draw guide lines.
3. Appliqué A, A-R, B, B-R, C, and C-R leaf pieces in alphabetical order onto the base fabric.
4. Appliqué D and D-R bud pieces onto the base fabric.
5. Appliqué pieces E and E-R onto No. 4.
6. Appliqué piece F and piece F-R.
7. Baste piece J and J-R onto the base fabric.
8. Appliqué piece G and piece G-R over the pieces that are basted in place onto No. 7.
9. Appliqué piece I and two H pieces, followed by I-R and two H-R pieces. Appliqué piece Q in the center.
10. Appliqué piece K and piece K-R.
11. Appliqué pieces L, L-R, M, and M-R onto No. 10.
12. Appliqué piece N.
13. Appliqué pieces O, O-R, and P onto No. 12.

Bracken

With bamboo baskets in hand, Japanese people search hill and dale every spring for bracken, a wild plant. Bracken puts its head above the ground with great vigor each spring and then grows very fast. A young bracken sprout is shaped like a fist and is sometimes called that. Though much larger, it looks similar to fiddlehead fern and is prized by gourmets in the same manner. Even a thousand years ago, Japanese people relished having bracken at their supper tables. The healthy-looking plant was favored by the people as a good-luck design for kimonos and furniture in ancient times. A small number of families eventually adopted the motif as a family crest. All the designs play up the curving nature of the stalks of the plant. Several of the variations show three fronds, either uncurling gracefully, or tightly wound into a coil. Some, like the pattern I have chosen, show several mature stalks of the plant gathered into a formal arrangement.

TO MAKE THE CREST

First cut the number of pieces indicated on the templates on pages 119 to 120. Sew the pieces together in the following sequence, using the diagram as a guide.

1. Cut a base square of background fabric measuring 14½" ¥ 14½" (37 cm ¥ 37 cm).
2. Lay out all of the templates on the base square and draw guide lines.
3. Appliqué pieces A, B, C, D, and E onto the base fabric in alphabetical order, followed by A-R, B-R, C-R, D-R, and E-R.
4. Appliqué F, G, H, I, and J in that order.
5. Appliqué two K pieces and two K-R pieces onto No. 4.

Finished block size: 14" ¥ 14" (36 cm ¥ 36 cm)

Nandina

The nandina is an evergreen shrub that grows to about six feet in height, sometimes taller. In the early summer it has white flowers. In the winter, its bright red fruit makes a pretty accent point in a snow scene. The red fruit is a symbol of long life because it stays on the branches for months. At New Year, flower arrangements in the alcoves of every house in Japan all contain nandina. The nandina found its way into the designs of family crests by the late feudal period. There are ten or so variations, some of which feature only the berry, others only the leaf. The majority, by far, show both the leaf and the berry. Memories of my childhood flooded my mind as I created a branch of lovely nandina with its assortment of red and green fruit. Playing house with those red fruits on a big leaf is a treasured recollection for me.

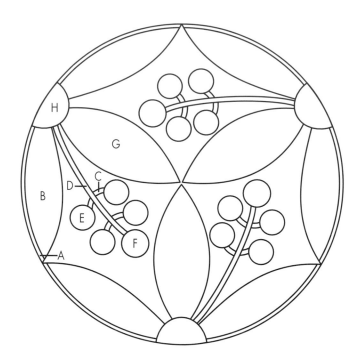

TO MAKE THE CREST

First cut the number of pieces indicated on the templates on page 121. Sew the pieces together in the following sequence, using the diagram as a guide.

1. Cut a base square of background fabric measuring 14½" ¥ 14½" (37 cm ¥ 37 cm).
2. Lay out all of the templates on the base square and draw guide lines.
3. Draw an 11" (28 cm) circle on the base fabric. Appliqué six A pieces along the circle.
4. Appliqué one B piece onto each A piece (a total of six).
5. Appliqué four C pieces onto the base. Appliqué one D piece over the C pieces. Appliqué one E piece onto each C piece and one F piece onto each D piece. Repeat twice.
6. Appliqué three G pieces in the center of the design.
7. Appliqué three H pieces as indicated in the diagram.

Finished block size: 14" ¥ 14" (36 cm ¥ 36 cm)

Nandina Quilt

To Make the Quilt

1. Cut four base squares of background fabric measuring 14½" ¥ 14½" (37 cm ¥ 37 cm).
2. Lay out all of the templates on the base squares and draw guide lines.
3. Appliqué two J pieces, pieces K and K-R, and six C pieces onto the background fabric.
4. Appliqué two H pieces onto the two J pieces.
5. Appliqué six E pieces and four D pieces onto the background fabric.
6. Sew pieces L, M, N, and O together. Make two units and appliqué onto the background fabric.
7. Sew piece B to P and piece B-R to P-R. Appliqué these units onto the background fabric.
8. Appliqué one I piece and three H pieces, as shown. Make four blocks total.
9. Sew the blocks together, as shown.
10. Attach the side borders.
11. Sew the corner squares to the top and bottom borders, then attach the borders to the quilt.

Quilt size	30" ¥ 30" (76 cm ¥ 76 cm)	
Block size	14" ¥ 14" (36 cm ¥ 36 cm)	
Setting	2 ¥ 2	
Blocks	4	

FABRIC AMOUNTS	YARDS	CM
Background squares	1	91
Template B	⅛	11
Template C	⅛	11
Template D	⅛	11
Template E	⅛	11
Template H	⅛	11
Template I	⅛	11
Template J	⅛	11
Template K	⅛	11
Template L	⅛	11
Template M	⅛	11
Template N	⅛	11
Template O	⅛	11
Template P	⅛	11
Border: 1" (2.5 cm)	⅛	11
Post: 1" ¥ 1" (2.5 cm ¥ 2.5 cm)	⅛	11

CUTTING	QUANTITY
Background squares: 14½" (37 cm)	4
Template B	8
Template C	24
Template D	16
Template E	32
Template H	20
Template I	4
Template J	8
Template K	8 (Reverse 4)
Template L	8
Template M	8
Template N	8
Template O	8
Template P	8 (Reverse 4)
Border: 1½" ¥ 29" (2.5 cm ¥ 73.6 cm)	4
Posts: 1½" ¥ 1½" (3.8 cm ¥ 3.8 cm)	4

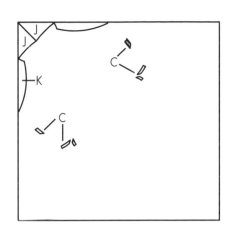

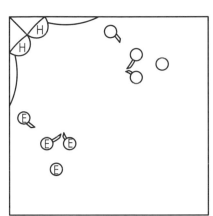

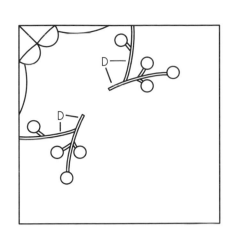

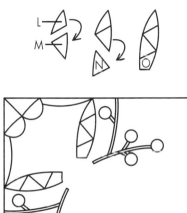

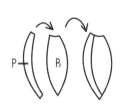

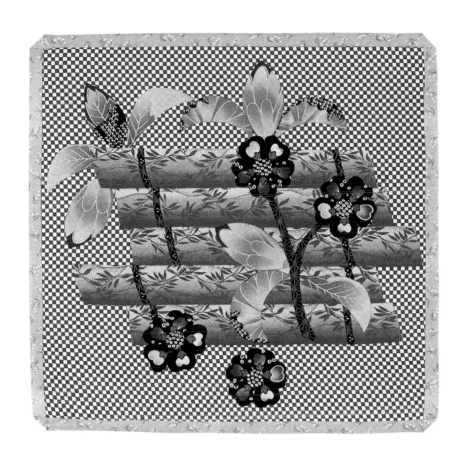

Templates

Peony

Note: Add ¼" (0.8 cm) seam allowance or less to all templates.

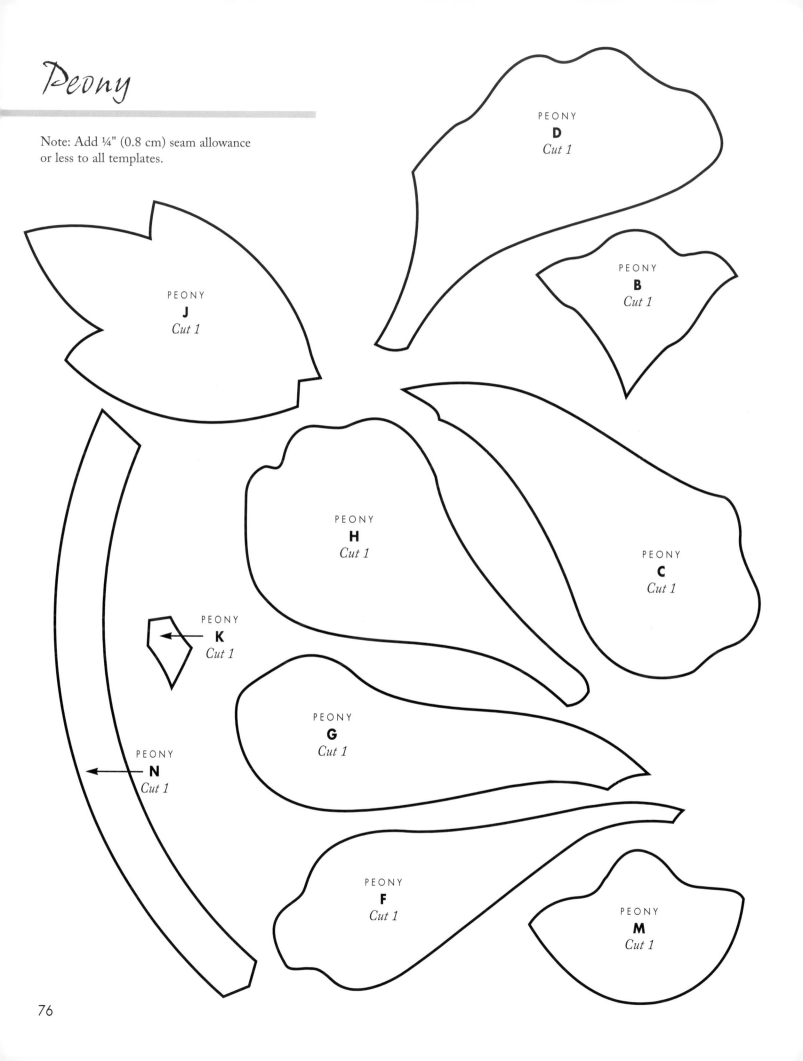

PEONY
D
Cut 1

PEONY
B
Cut 1

PEONY
J
Cut 1

PEONY
H
Cut 1

PEONY
C
Cut 1

PEONY
K
Cut 1

PEONY
G
Cut 1

PEONY
N
Cut 1

PEONY
F
Cut 1

PEONY
M
Cut 1

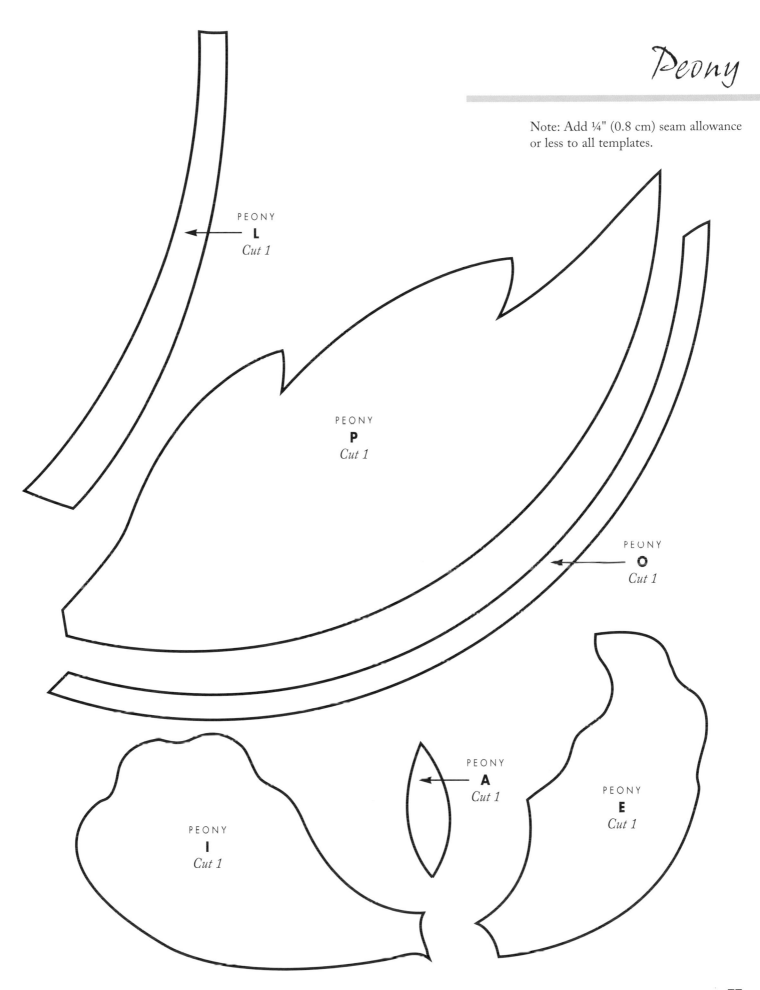

Note: Add ¼" (0.8 cm) seam allowance
or less to all templates.

PEONY
L
Cut 1

PEONY
P
Cut 1

PEONY
O
Cut 1

PEONY
A
Cut 1

PEONY
I
Cut 1

PEONY
E
Cut 1

Cherry Blossoms on a Tanzaku

Note: Add ¼" (0.8 cm) seam allowance or less to all templates.

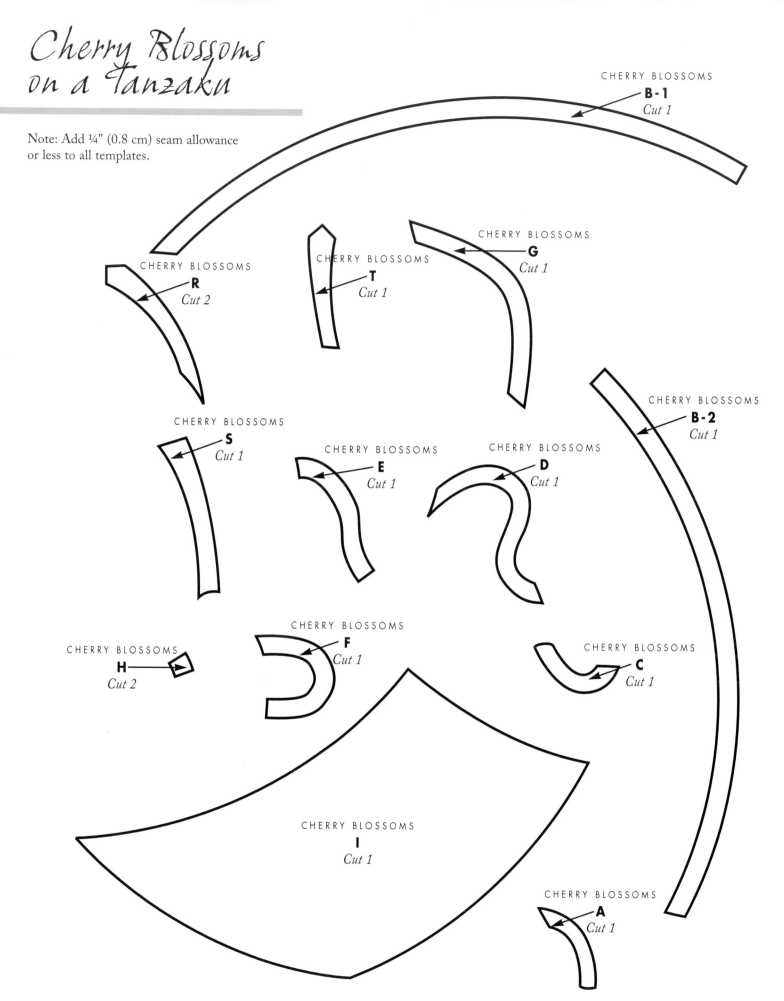

CHERRY BLOSSOMS
B-1
Cut 1

CHERRY BLOSSOMS
G
Cut 1

CHERRY BLOSSOMS
R
Cut 2

CHERRY BLOSSOMS
T
Cut 1

CHERRY BLOSSOMS
B-2
Cut 1

CHERRY BLOSSOMS
S
Cut 1

CHERRY BLOSSOMS
E
Cut 1

CHERRY BLOSSOMS
D
Cut 1

CHERRY BLOSSOMS
H
Cut 2

CHERRY BLOSSOMS
F
Cut 1

CHERRY BLOSSOMS
C
Cut 1

CHERRY BLOSSOMS
I
Cut 1

CHERRY BLOSSOMS
A
Cut 1

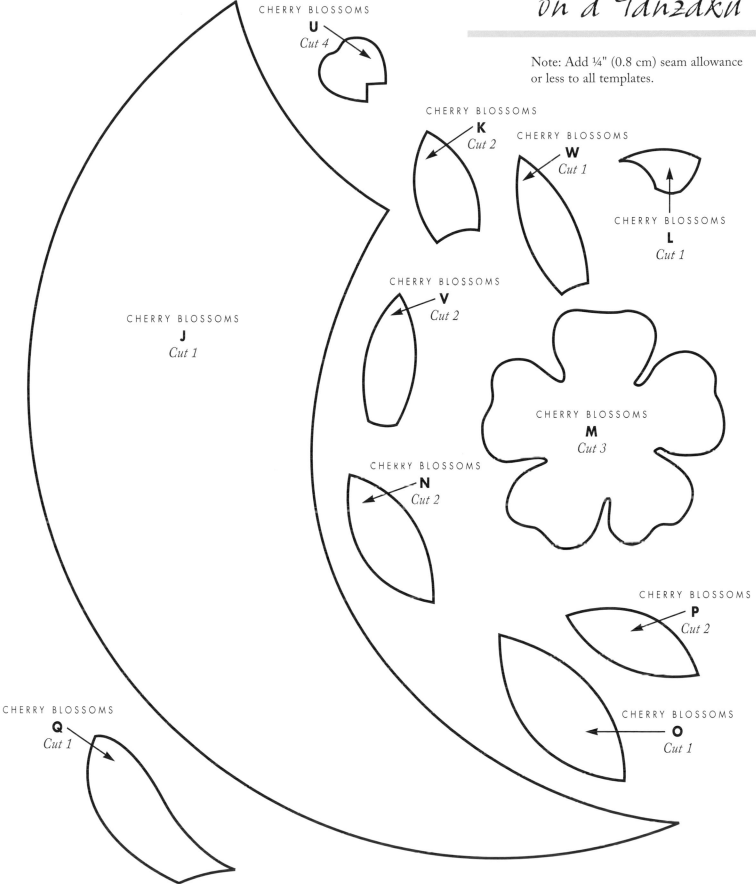

Cherry Blossoms
on a Tanzaku

Note: Add ¼" (0.8 cm) seam allowance
or less to all templates.

CHERRY BLOSSOMS
U
Cut 4

CHERRY BLOSSOMS
K
Cut 2

CHERRY BLOSSOMS
W
Cut 1

CHERRY BLOSSOMS
L
Cut 1

CHERRY BLOSSOMS
V
Cut 2

CHERRY BLOSSOMS
J
Cut 1

CHERRY BLOSSOMS
M
Cut 3

CHERRY BLOSSOMS
N
Cut 2

CHERRY BLOSSOMS
P
Cut 2

CHERRY BLOSSOMS
O
Cut 1

CHERRY BLOSSOMS
Q
Cut 1

Wood Sorrel

Note: Add ¼" (0.8 cm) seam allowance or less to all templates.

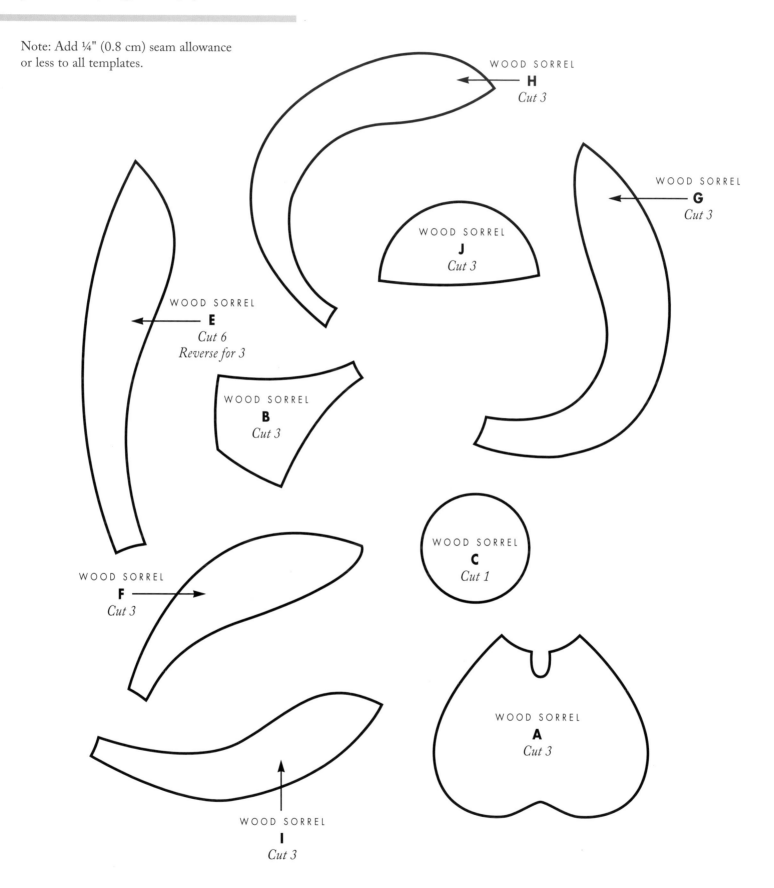

WOOD SORREL
H
Cut 3

WOOD SORREL
G
Cut 3

WOOD SORREL
J
Cut 3

WOOD SORREL
E
Cut 6
Reverse for 3

WOOD SORREL
B
Cut 3

WOOD SORREL
F
Cut 3

WOOD SORREL
C
Cut 1

WOOD SORREL
A
Cut 3

WOOD SORREL
I
Cut 3

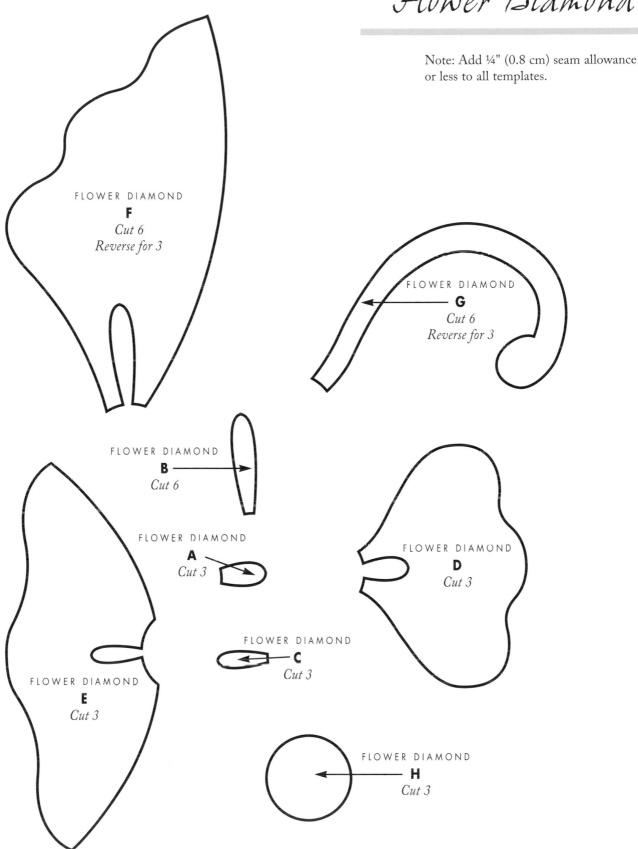

Note: Add ¼" (0.8 cm) seam allowance or less to all templates.

FLOWER DIAMOND
F
Cut 6
Reverse for 3

FLOWER DIAMOND
G
Cut 6
Reverse for 3

FLOWER DIAMOND
B
Cut 6

FLOWER DIAMOND
A
Cut 3

FLOWER DIAMOND
D
Cut 3

FLOWER DIAMOND
C
Cut 3

FLOWER DIAMOND
E
Cut 3

FLOWER DIAMOND
H
Cut 3

Gingko

Note: Add ¼" (0.8 cm) seam allowance or less to all templates.

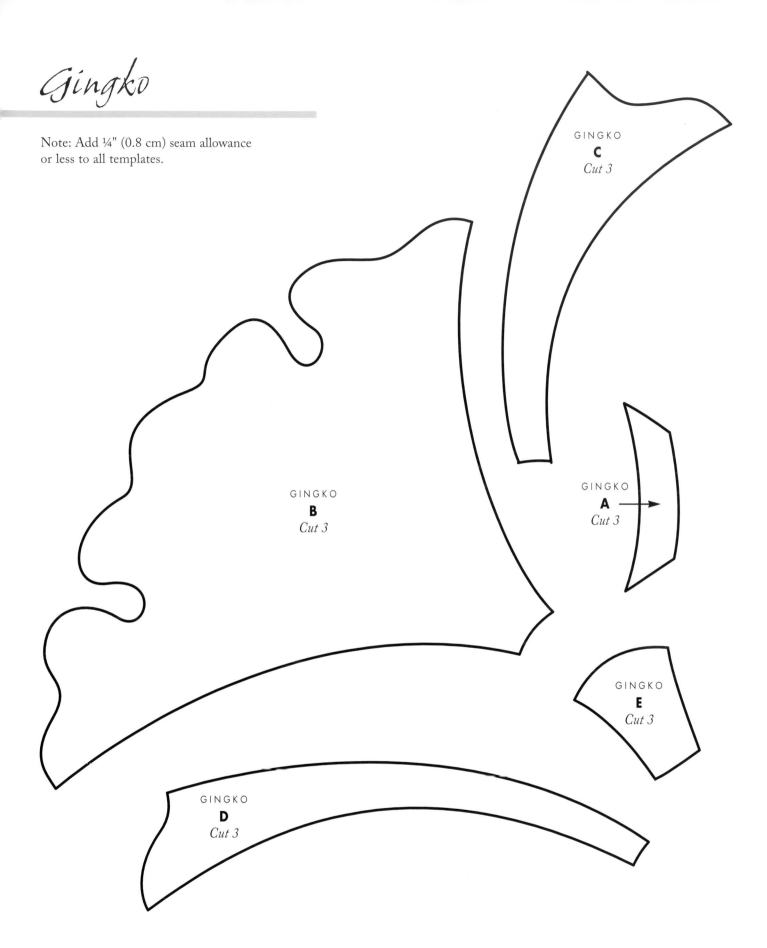

GINGKO
C
Cut 3

GINGKO
B
Cut 3

GINGKO
A
Cut 3

GINGKO
E
Cut 3

GINGKO
D
Cut 3

Butterfly Wheel

Note: Add ¼" (0.8 cm) seam allowance or less to all templates.

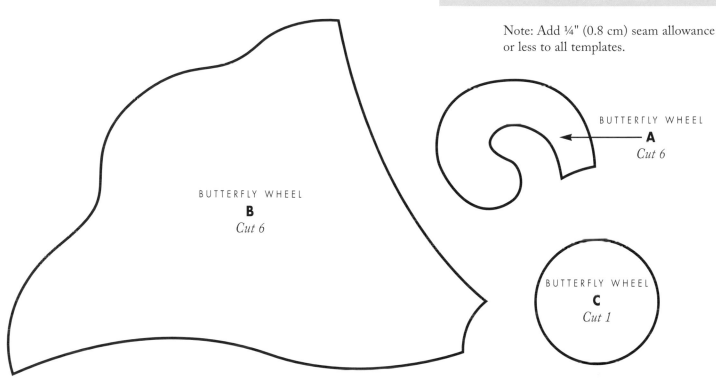

BUTTERFLY WHEEL
A
Cut 6

BUTTERFLY WHEEL
B
Cut 6

BUTTERFLY WHEEL
C
Cut 1

Maple

Note: Add ¼" (0.8 cm) seam allowance or less to all templates.

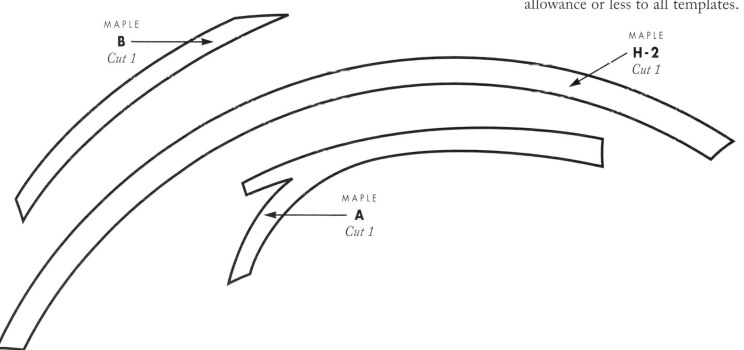

MAPLE
B
Cut 1

MAPLE
H-2
Cut 1

MAPLE
A
Cut 1

Maple

Note: Add ¼" (0.8 cm) seam allowance or less to all templates.

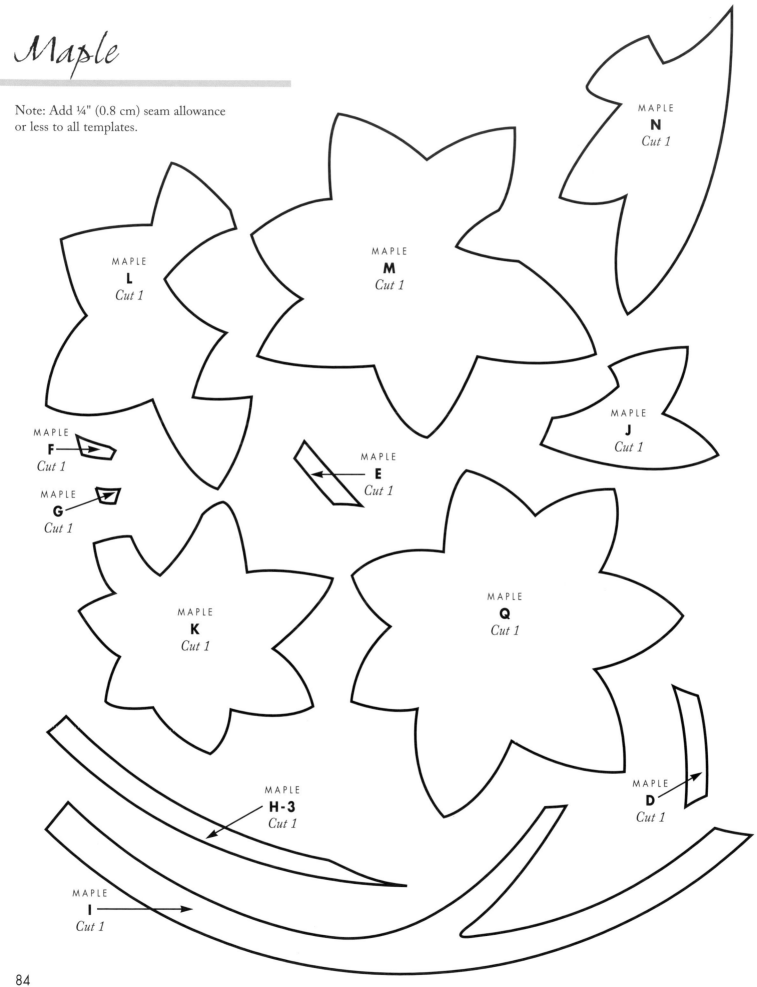

MAPLE
N
Cut 1

MAPLE
L
Cut 1

MAPLE
M
Cut 1

MAPLE
J
Cut 1

MAPLE
F
Cut 1

MAPLE
G
Cut 1

MAPLE
E
Cut 1

MAPLE
K
Cut 1

MAPLE
Q
Cut 1

MAPLE
D
Cut 1

MAPLE
H-3
Cut 1

MAPLE
I
Cut 1

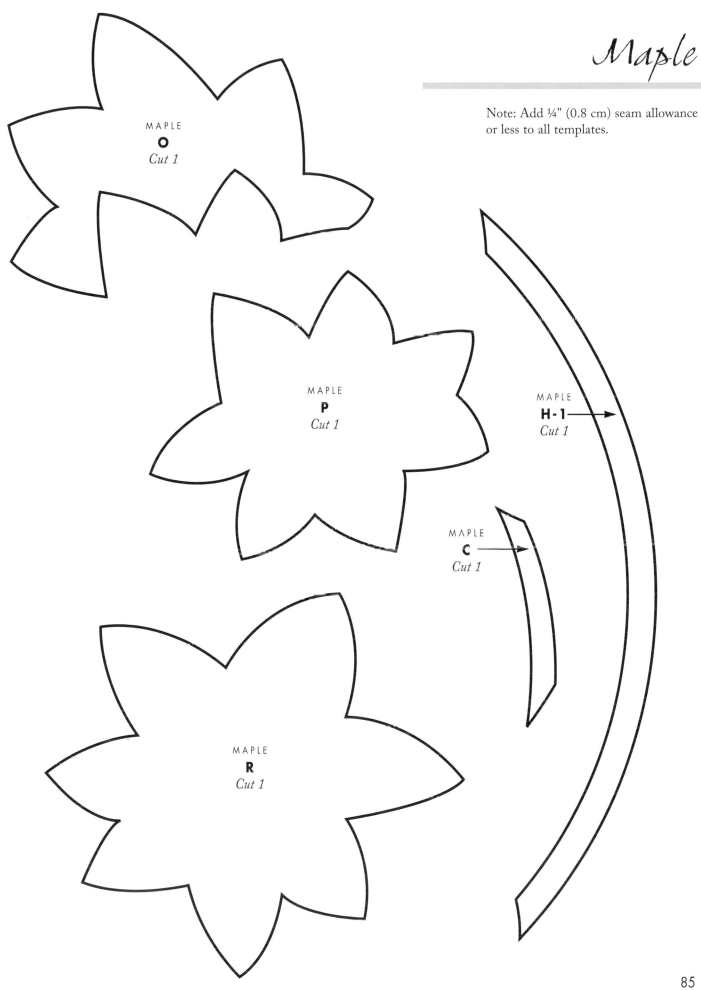

Note: Add ¼" (0.8 cm) seam allowance
or less to all templates.

MAPLE
O
Cut 1

MAPLE
P
Cut 1

MAPLE
H-1
Cut 1

MAPLE
C
Cut 1

MAPLE
R
Cut 1

Wisteria Variation

Note: Add ¼" (0.8 cm) seam allowance
or less to all templates.

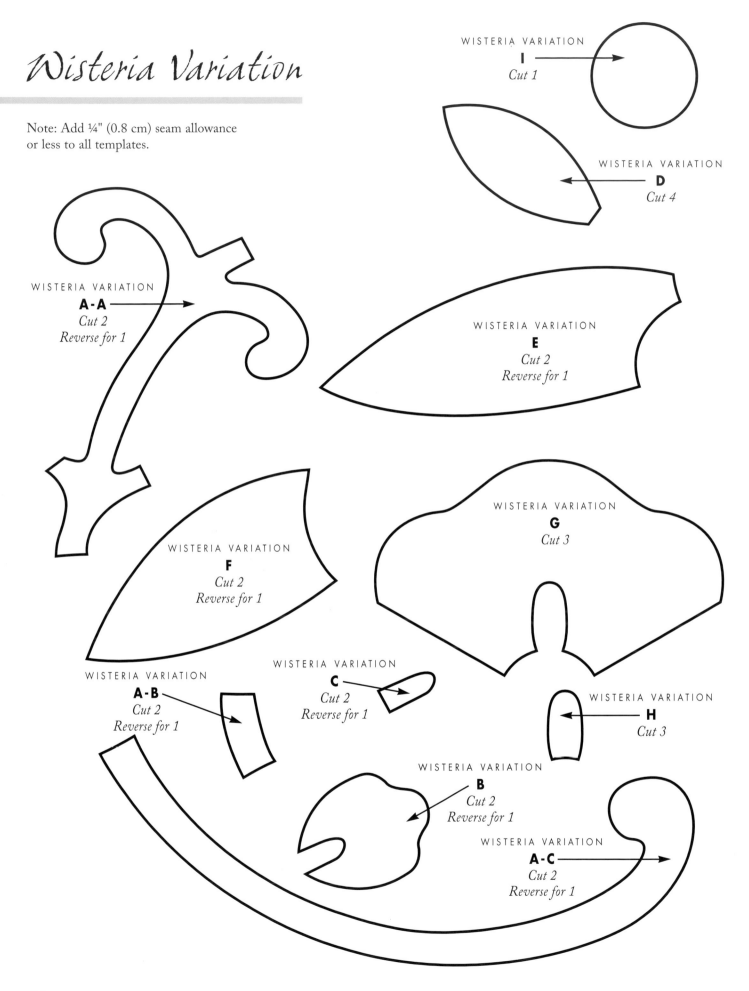

WISTERIA VARIATION
I
Cut 1

WISTERIA VARIATION
D
Cut 4

WISTERIA VARIATION
A-A
Cut 2
Reverse for 1

WISTERIA VARIATION
E
Cut 2
Reverse for 1

WISTERIA VARIATION
F
Cut 2
Reverse for 1

WISTERIA VARIATION
G
Cut 3

WISTERIA VARIATION
A-B
Cut 2
Reverse for 1

WISTERIA VARIATION
C
Cut 2
Reverse for 1

WISTERIA VARIATION
H
Cut 3

WISTERIA VARIATION
B
Cut 2
Reverse for 1

WISTERIA VARIATION
A-C
Cut 2
Reverse for 1

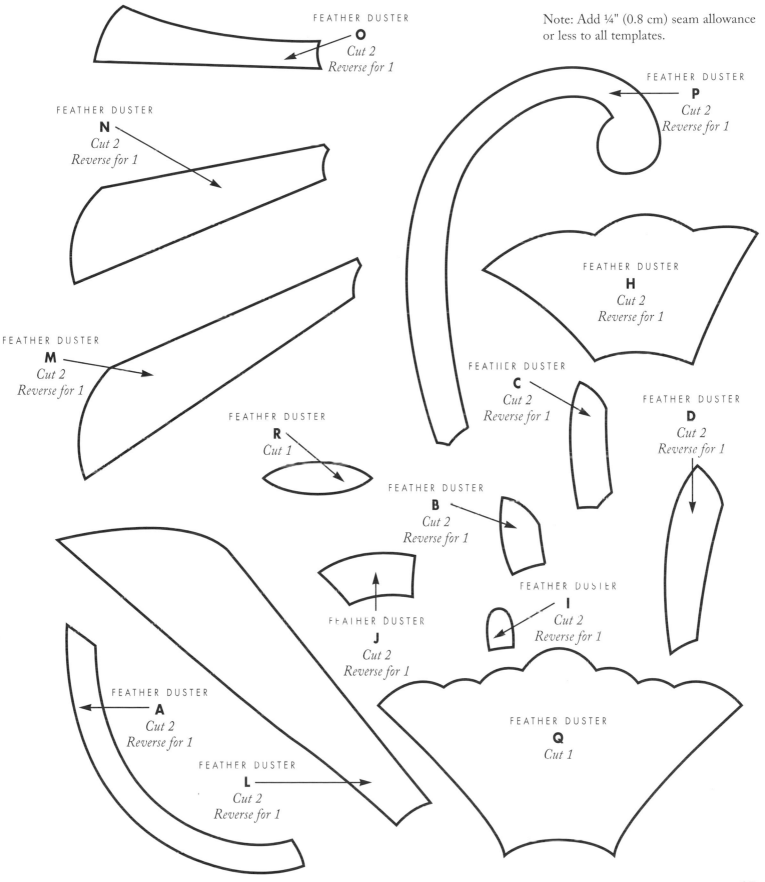

Feather Duster

FEATHER DUSTER
O
Cut 2
Reverse for 1

Note: Add ¼" (0.8 cm) seam allowance or less to all templates.

FEATHER DUSTER
P
Cut 2
Reverse for 1

FEATHER DUSTER
N
Cut 2
Reverse for 1

FEATHER DUSTER
H
Cut 2
Reverse for 1

FEATHER DUSTER
M
Cut 2
Reverse for 1

FEATHER DUSTER
C
Cut 2
Reverse for 1

FEATHER DUSTER
D
Cut 2
Reverse for 1

FEATHER DUSTER
R
Cut 1

FEATHER DUSTER
B
Cut 2
Reverse for 1

FEATHER DUSTER
I
Cut 2
Reverse for 1

FEATHER DUSTER
J
Cut 2
Reverse for 1

FEATHER DUSTER
A
Cut 2
Reverse for 1

FEATHER DUSTER
Q
Cut 1

FEATHER DUSTER
L
Cut 2
Reverse for 1

Feather Duster

Note: Add ¼" (0.8 cm) seam allowance or less to all templates.

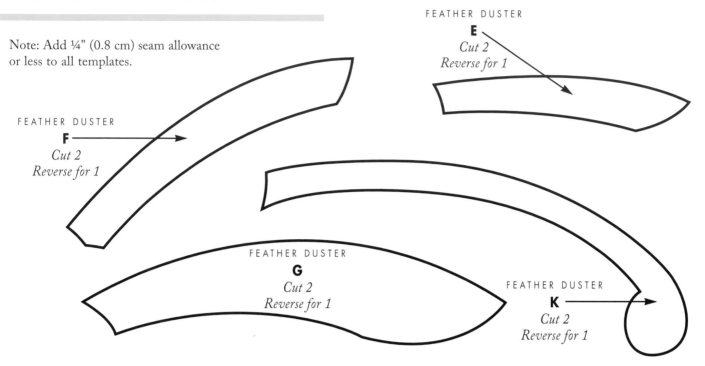

FEATHER DUSTER
E
Cut 2
Reverse for 1

FEATHER DUSTER
F
Cut 2
Reverse for 1

FEATHER DUSTER
G
Cut 2
Reverse for 1

FEATHER DUSTER
K
Cut 2
Reverse for 1

Plum Blossom

Note: Add ¼" (0.8 cm) seam allowance or less to all templates.

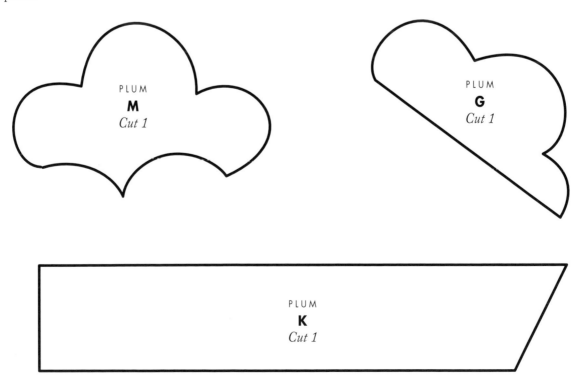

PLUM
M
Cut 1

PLUM
G
Cut 1

PLUM
K
Cut 1

Plum Blossom

Note: Add ¼" (0.8 cm) seam allowance or less to all templates.

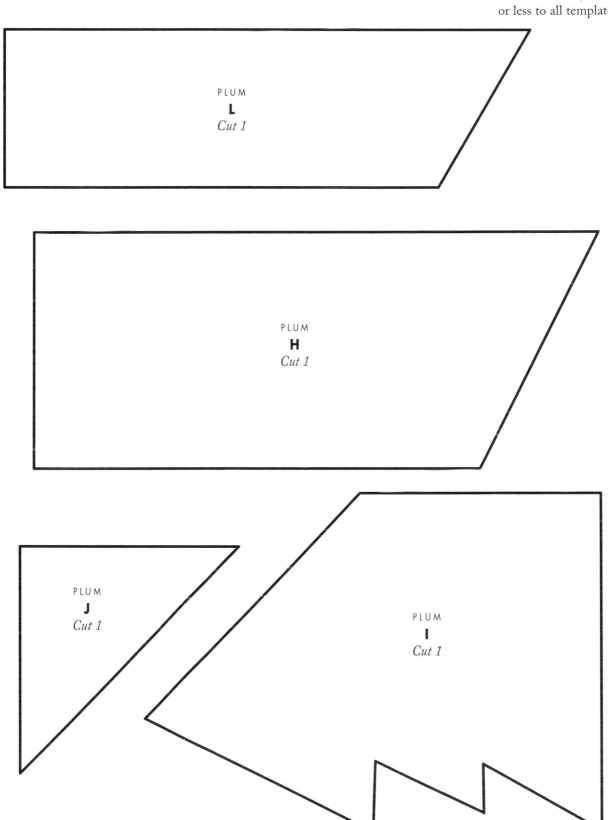

PLUM
L
Cut 1

PLUM
H
Cut 1

PLUM
J
Cut 1

PLUM
I
Cut 1

Plum Blossom

Note: Add ¼" (0.8 cm) seam allowance or less to all templates.

PIGEONS
A
Cut 2
Reverse for 1

Note: Add ¼" (0.8 cm) seam allowance
or less to all templates.

PIGEONS
D
Cut 2
Reverse for 1

PIGEONS
B
Cut 2
Reverse for 1

PIGEONS
C
Cut 2
Reverse for 1

PIGEONS
H
Cut 2
Reverse for 1

PIGEONS
G
Cut 2
Reverse for 1

PIGEONS
F
Cut 2
Reverse for 1

PIGEONS
E
Cut 2
Reverse for 1

91

Gentian

Note: Add ¼" (0.8 cm) seam allowance
or less to all templates.

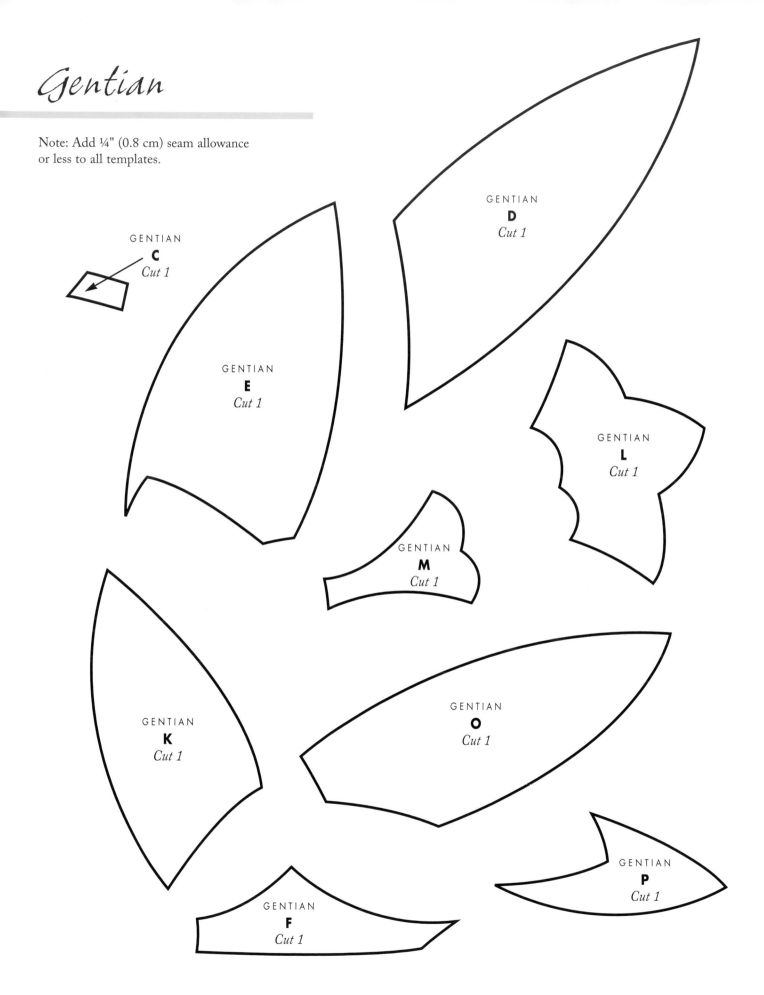

GENTIAN
C
Cut 1

GENTIAN
D
Cut 1

GENTIAN
E
Cut 1

GENTIAN
L
Cut 1

GENTIAN
M
Cut 1

GENTIAN
K
Cut 1

GENTIAN
O
Cut 1

GENTIAN
P
Cut 1

GENTIAN
F
Cut 1

Gentian

Note: Add ¼" (0.8 cm) seam allowance or less to all templates.

GENTIAN
H
Cut 1

GENTIAN
I
Cut 2
Reverse for 1

GENTIAN
G
Cut 1

GENTIAN
A
Cut 1

GENTIAN
J
Cut 2
Reverse for 1

GENTIAN
N
Cut 1

GENTIAN
S
Cut 1

GENTIAN
C
Cut 1

GENTIAN
R
Cut 2
Reverse for 1

GENTIAN
Q
Cut 1

GENTIAN
T
Cut 2
Reverse for 1

Noshi

Note: Add ¼" (0.8 cm) seam allowance
or less to all templates.

NOSHI
N
Cut 1

NOSHI
M
Cut 1

NOSHI
J
Cut 1

NOSHI
I
Cut 1

NOSHI
L
Cut 1

NOSHI
K
Cut 1

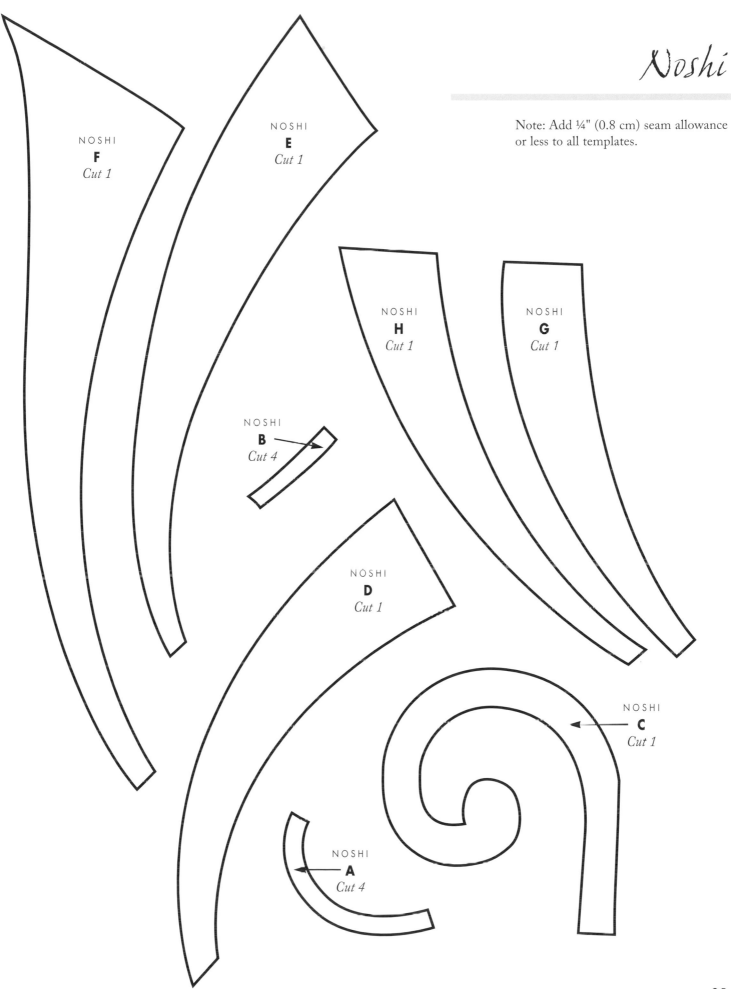

Noshi

Note: Add ¼" (0.8 cm) seam allowance or less to all templates.

NOSHI
F
Cut 1

NOSHI
E
Cut 1

NOSHI
H
Cut 1

NOSHI
G
Cut 1

NOSHI
B
Cut 4

NOSHI
D
Cut 1

NOSHI
C
Cut 1

NOSHI
A
Cut 4

Chrysanthemum

Note: Add ¼" (0.8 cm) seam allowance or less to all templates.

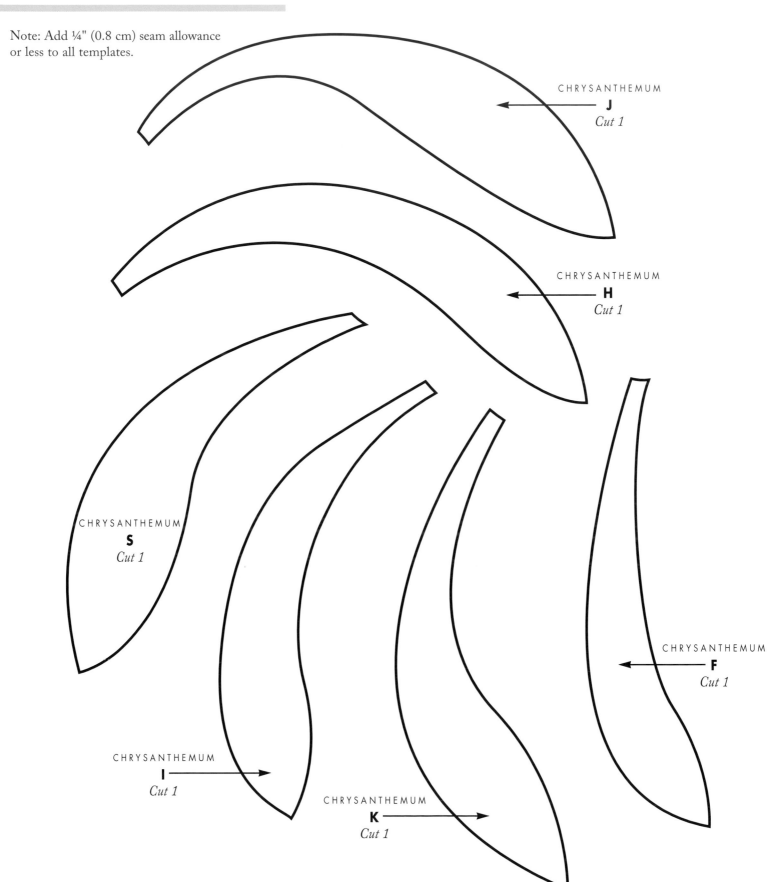

CHRYSANTHEMUM
J
Cut 1

CHRYSANTHEMUM
H
Cut 1

CHRYSANTHEMUM
S
Cut 1

CHRYSANTHEMUM
F
Cut 1

CHRYSANTHEMUM
I
Cut 1

CHRYSANTHEMUM
K
Cut 1

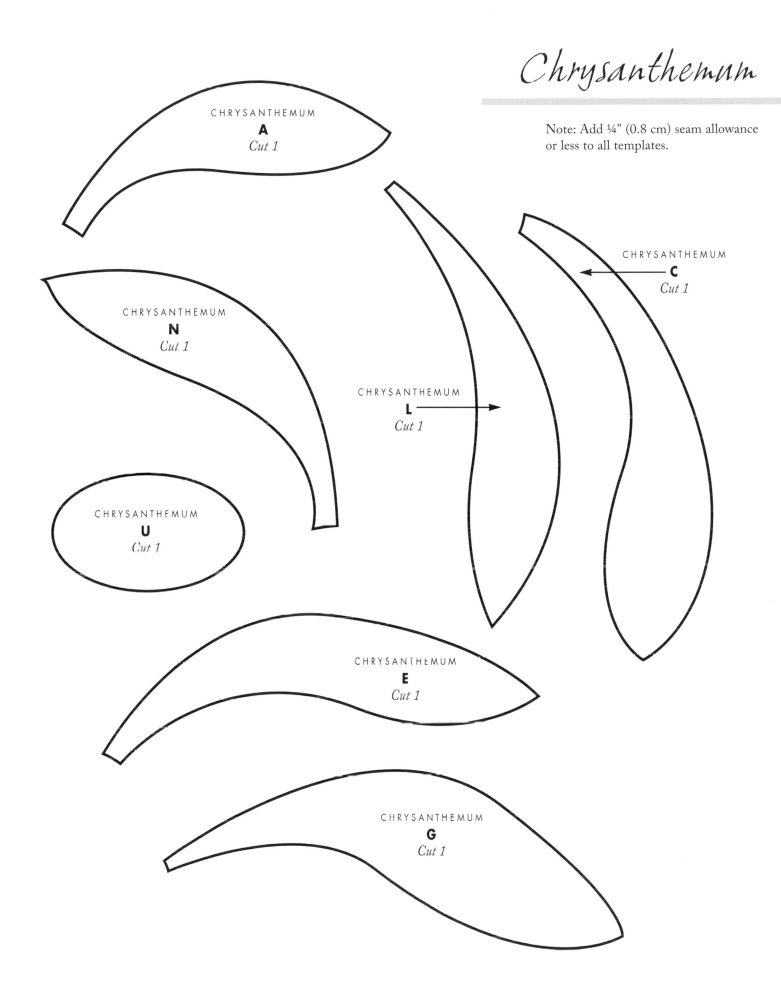

Chrysanthemum

Note: Add ¼" (0.8 cm) seam allowance or less to all templates.

CHRYSANTHEMUM
A
Cut 1

CHRYSANTHEMUM
C
Cut 1

CHRYSANTHEMUM
N
Cut 1

CHRYSANTHEMUM
L
Cut 1

CHRYSANTHEMUM
U
Cut 1

CHRYSANTHEMUM
E
Cut 1

CHRYSANTHEMUM
G
Cut 1

Chrysanthemum

Note: Add ¼" (0.8 cm) seam allowance or less to all templates.

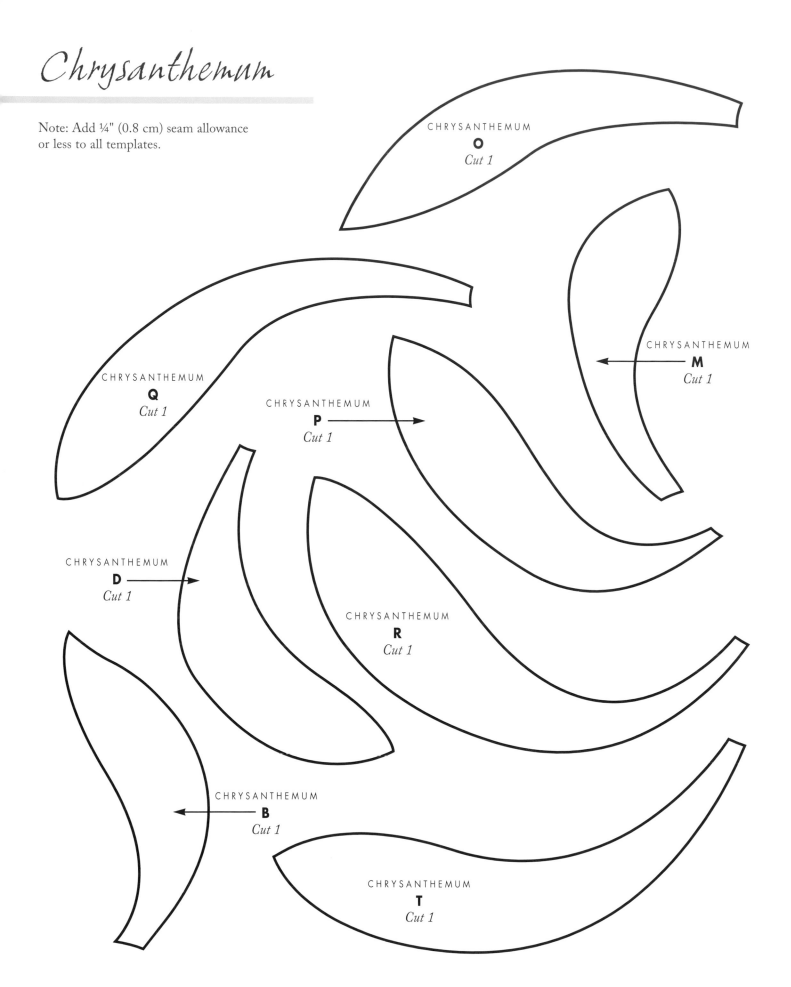

CHRYSANTHEMUM
O
Cut 1

CHRYSANTHEMUM
M
Cut 1

CHRYSANTHEMUM
Q
Cut 1

CHRYSANTHEMUM
P
Cut 1

CHRYSANTHEMUM
D
Cut 1

CHRYSANTHEMUM
R
Cut 1

CHRYSANTHEMUM
B
Cut 1

CHRYSANTHEMUM
T
Cut 1

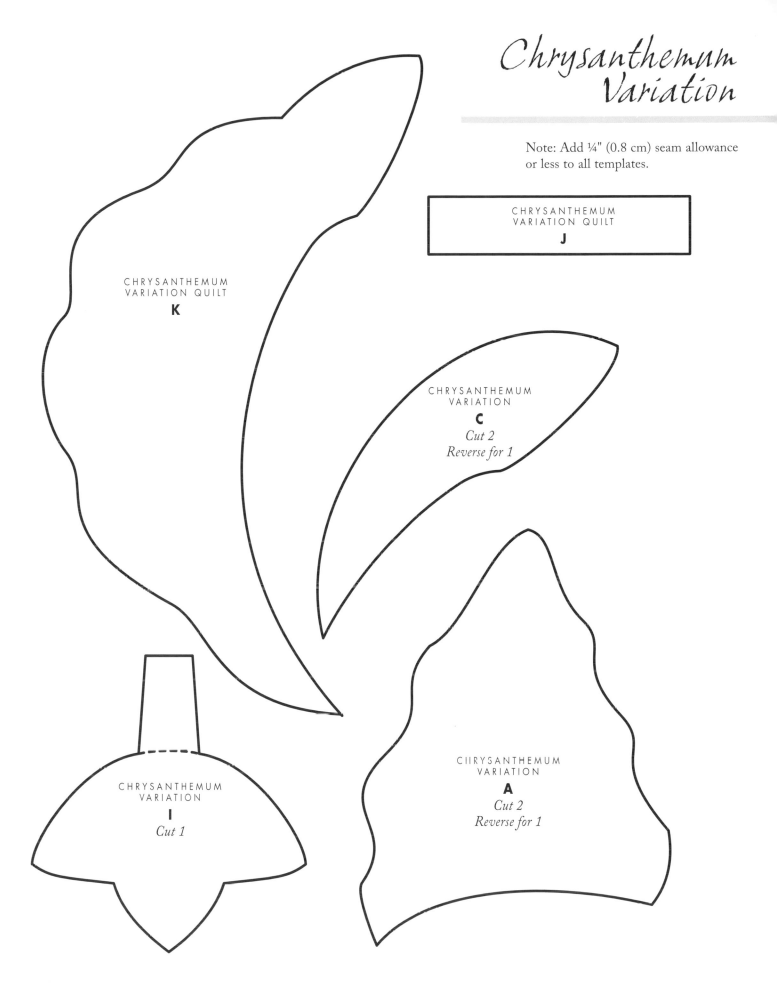

Chrysanthemum Variation

Note: Add ¼" (0.8 cm) seam allowance or less to all templates.

CHRYSANTHEMUM
VARIATION QUILT
J

CHRYSANTHEMUM
VARIATION QUILT
K

CHRYSANTHEMUM
VARIATION
C
Cut 2
Reverse for 1

CHRYSANTHEMUM
VARIATION
I
Cut 1

CIIRYSANTHEMUM
VARIATION
A
Cut 2
Reverse for 1

Chrysanthemum Variation

Note: Add ¼" (0.8 cm) seam allowance
or less to all templates.

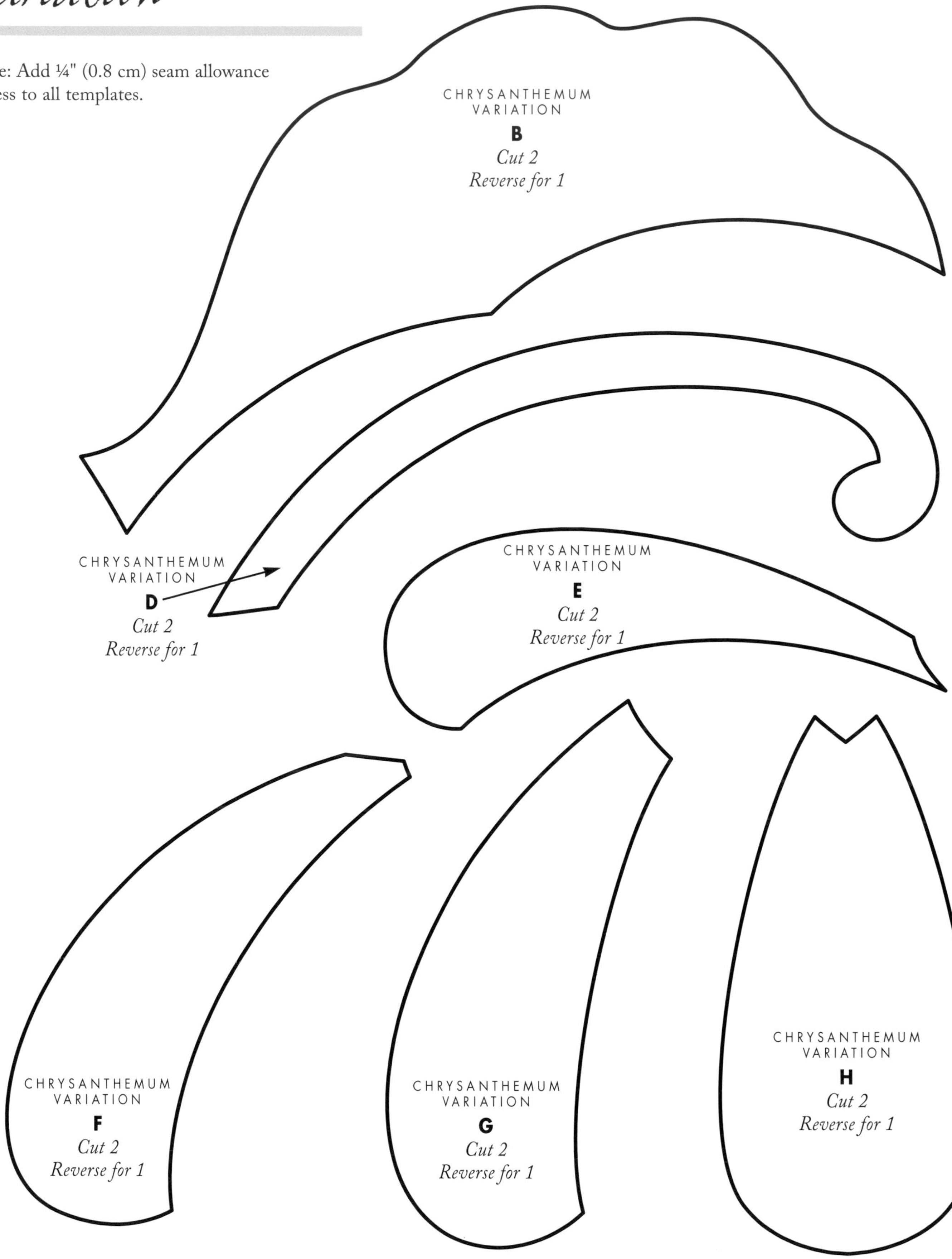

CHRYSANTHEMUM
VARIATION
B
Cut 2
Reverse for 1

CHRYSANTHEMUM
VARIATION
D
Cut 2
Reverse for 1

CHRYSANTHEMUM
VARIATION
E
Cut 2
Reverse for 1

CHRYSANTHEMUM
VARIATION
F
Cut 2
Reverse for 1

CHRYSANTHEMUM
VARIATION
G
Cut 2
Reverse for 1

CHRYSANTHEMUM
VARIATION
H
Cut 2
Reverse for 1

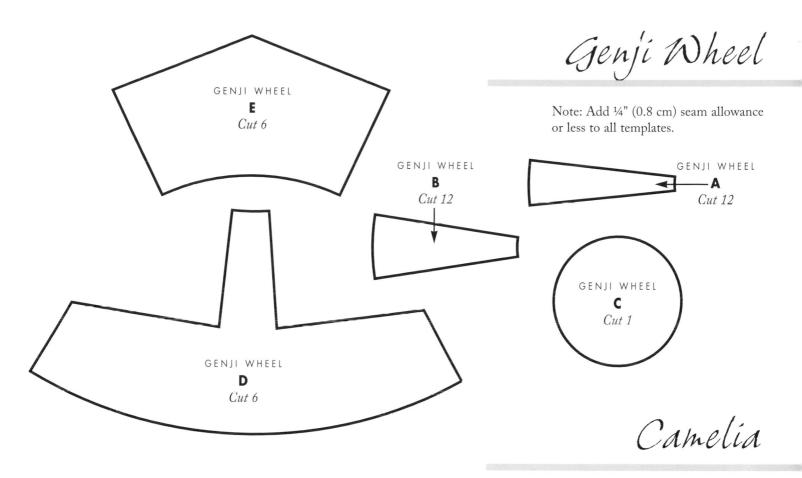

GENJI WHEEL
E
Cut 6

GENJI WHEEL
B
Cut 12

GENJI WHEEL
A
Cut 12

Note: Add ¼" (0.8 cm) seam allowance
or less to all templates.

GENJI WHEEL
C
Cut 1

GENJI WHEEL
D
Cut 6

Camelia

Note: Add ¼" (0.8 cm) seam allowance
or less to all templates.

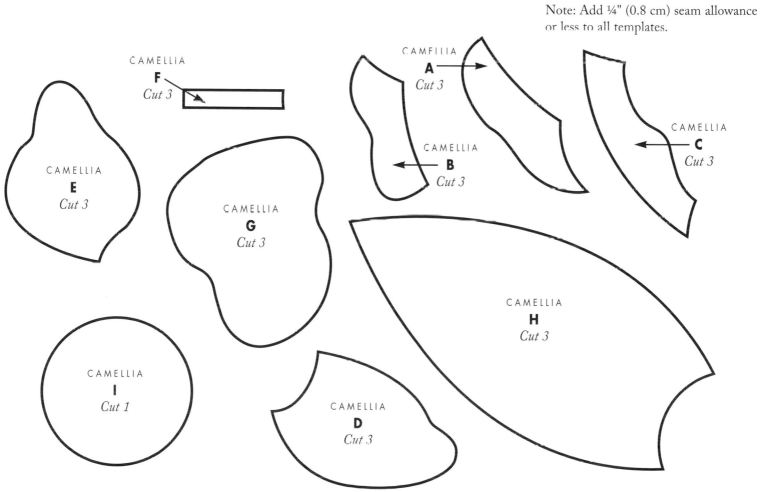

CAMELLIA
F
Cut 3

CAMELLIA
A
Cut 3

CAMELLIA
B
Cut 3

CAMELLIA
C
Cut 3

CAMELLIA
E
Cut 3

CAMELLIA
G
Cut 3

CAMELLIA
H
Cut 3

CAMELLIA
I
Cut 1

CAMELLIA
D
Cut 3

Sparrow in a Bamboo Cottage

Note: Add ¼" (0.8 cm) seam allowance
or less to all templates.

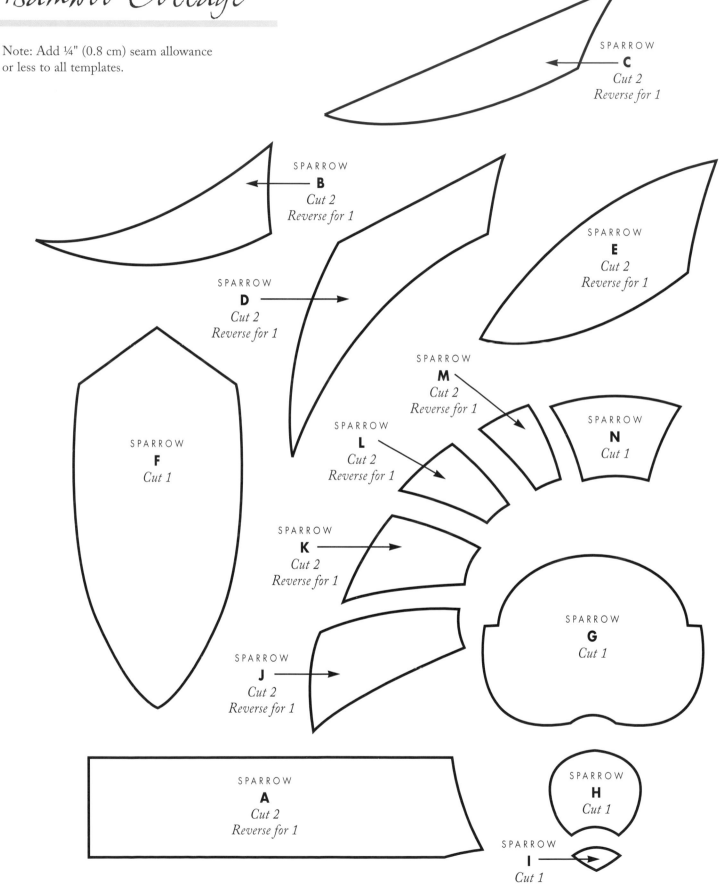

SPARROW
C
Cut 2
Reverse for 1

SPARROW
B
Cut 2
Reverse for 1

SPARROW
D
Cut 2
Reverse for 1

SPARROW
E
Cut 2
Reverse for 1

SPARROW
M
Cut 2
Reverse for 1

SPARROW
L
Cut 2
Reverse for 1

SPARROW
N
Cut 1

SPARROW
F
Cut 1

SPARROW
K
Cut 2
Reverse for 1

SPARROW
G
Cut 1

SPARROW
J
Cut 2
Reverse for 1

SPARROW
A
Cut 2
Reverse for 1

SPARROW
H
Cut 1

SPARROW
I
Cut 1

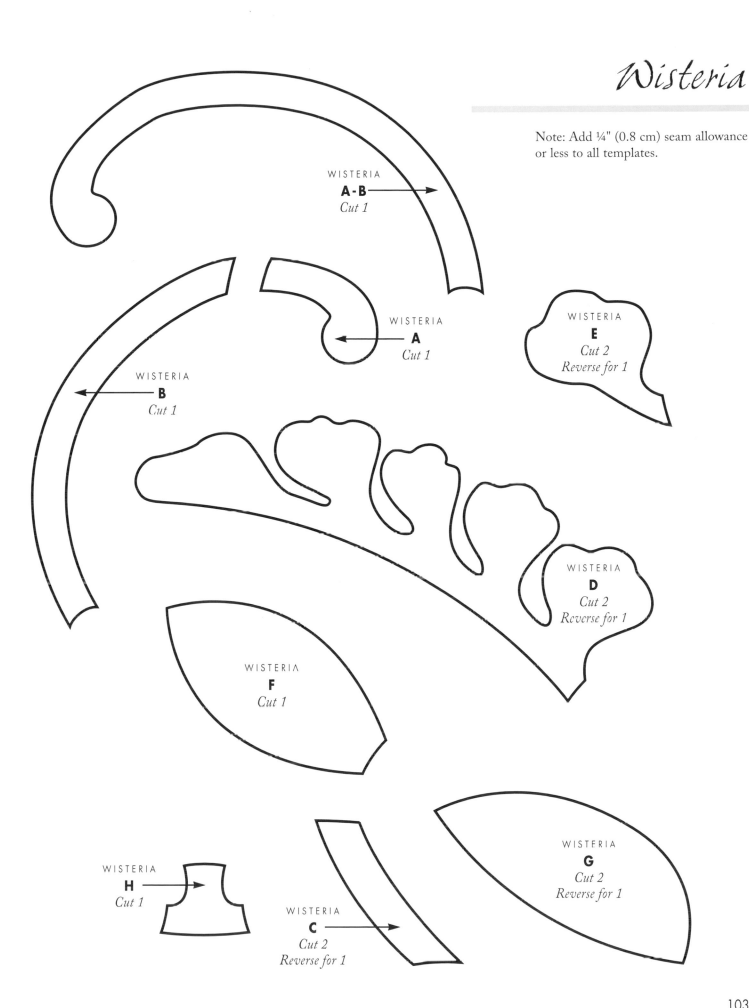

Wisteria

Note: Add ¼" (0.8 cm) seam allowance or less to all templates.

WISTERIA
A-B
Cut 1

WISTERIA
A
Cut 1

WISTERIA
B
Cut 1

WISTERIA
E
Cut 2
Reverse for 1

WISTERIA
D
Cut 2
Reverse for 1

WISTERIA
F
Cut 1

WISTERIA
G
Cut 2
Reverse for 1

WISTERIA
H
Cut 1

WISTERIA
C
Cut 2
Reverse for 1

103

Wild Mandarin

Note: Add ¼" (0.8 cm) seam allowance
or less to all templates.

MANDARIN QUILT
BACKGROUND

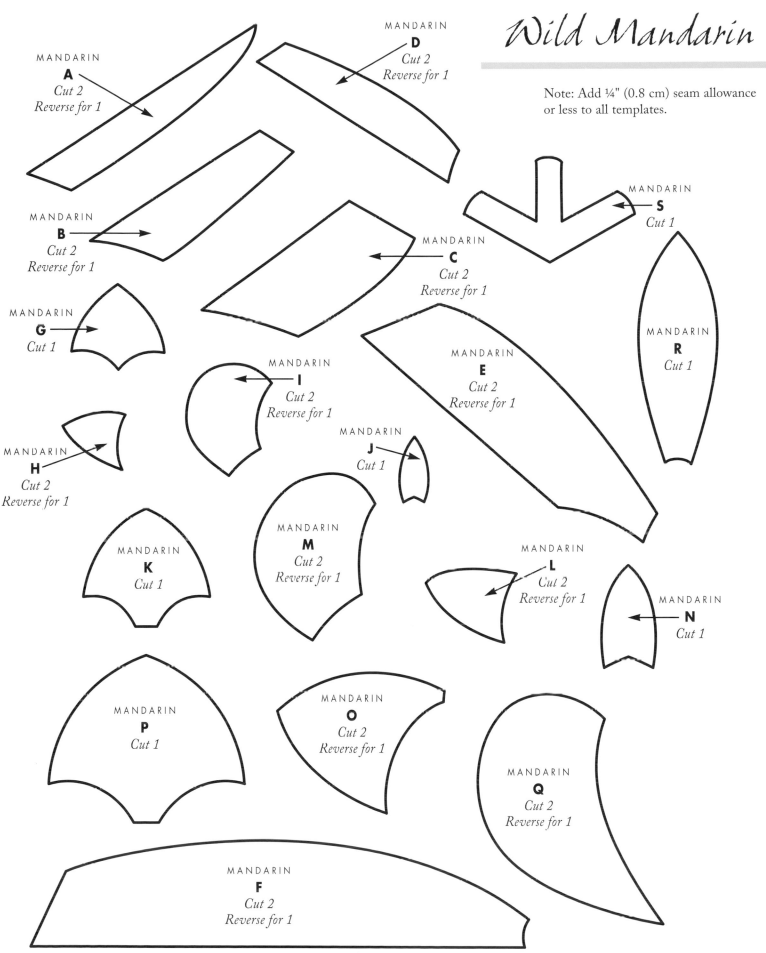

MANDARIN
A
Cut 2
Reverse for 1

MANDARIN
D
Cut 2
Reverse for 1

Wild Mandarin

Note: Add ¼" (0.8 cm) seam allowance
or less to all templates.

MANDARIN
B
Cut 2
Reverse for 1

MANDARIN
C
Cut 2
Reverse for 1

MANDARIN
S
Cut 1

MANDARIN
G
Cut 1

MANDARIN
I
Cut 2
Reverse for 1

MANDARIN
E
Cut 2
Reverse for 1

MANDARIN
R
Cut 1

MANDARIN
H
Cut 2
Reverse for 1

MANDARIN
J
Cut 1

MANDARIN
K
Cut 1

MANDARIN
M
Cut 2
Reverse for 1

MANDARIN
L
Cut 2
Reverse for 1

MANDARIN
N
Cut 1

MANDARIN
P
Cut 1

MANDARIN
O
Cut 2
Reverse for 1

MANDARIN
Q
Cut 2
Reverse for 1

MANDARIN
F
Cut 2
Reverse for 1

Wild Mandarin

Note: Add ¼" (0.8 cm) seam allowance or less to all templates.

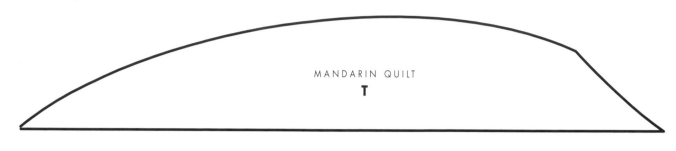

MANDARIN QUILT
T

MANDARIN QUILT
U

Mamezo Doll

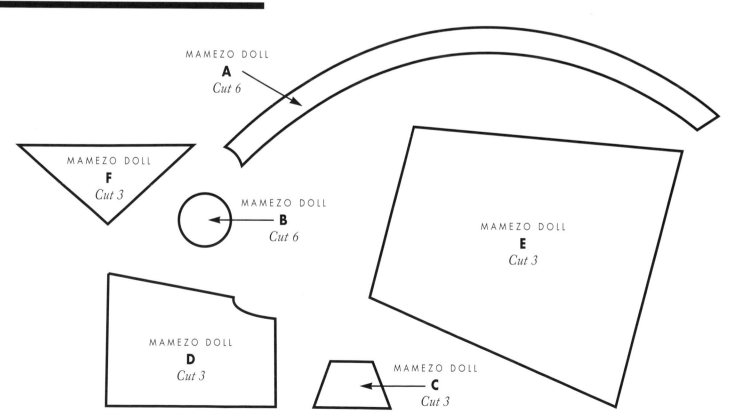

MAMEZO DOLL
A
Cut 6

MAMEZO DOLL
F
Cut 3

MAMEZO DOLL
B
Cut 6

MAMEZO DOLL
E
Cut 3

MAMEZO DOLL
D
Cut 3

MAMEZO DOLL
C
Cut 3

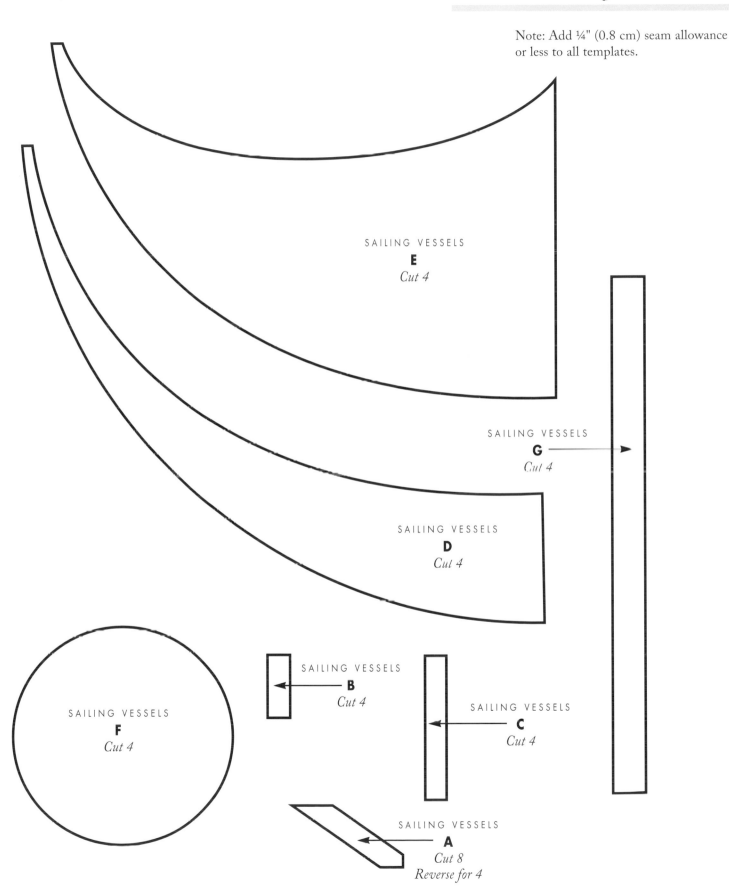

Sailing Vessels

Note: Add ¼" (0.8 cm) seam allowance or less to all templates.

SAILING VESSELS
E
Cut 4

SAILING VESSELS
G
Cut 4

SAILING VESSELS
D
Cut 4

SAILING VESSELS
F
Cut 4

SAILING VESSELS
B
Cut 4

SAILING VESSELS
C
Cut 4

SAILING VESSELS
A
Cut 8
Reverse for 4

Shinto Pendant

Note: Add ¼" (0.8 cm) seam allowance
or less to all templates.

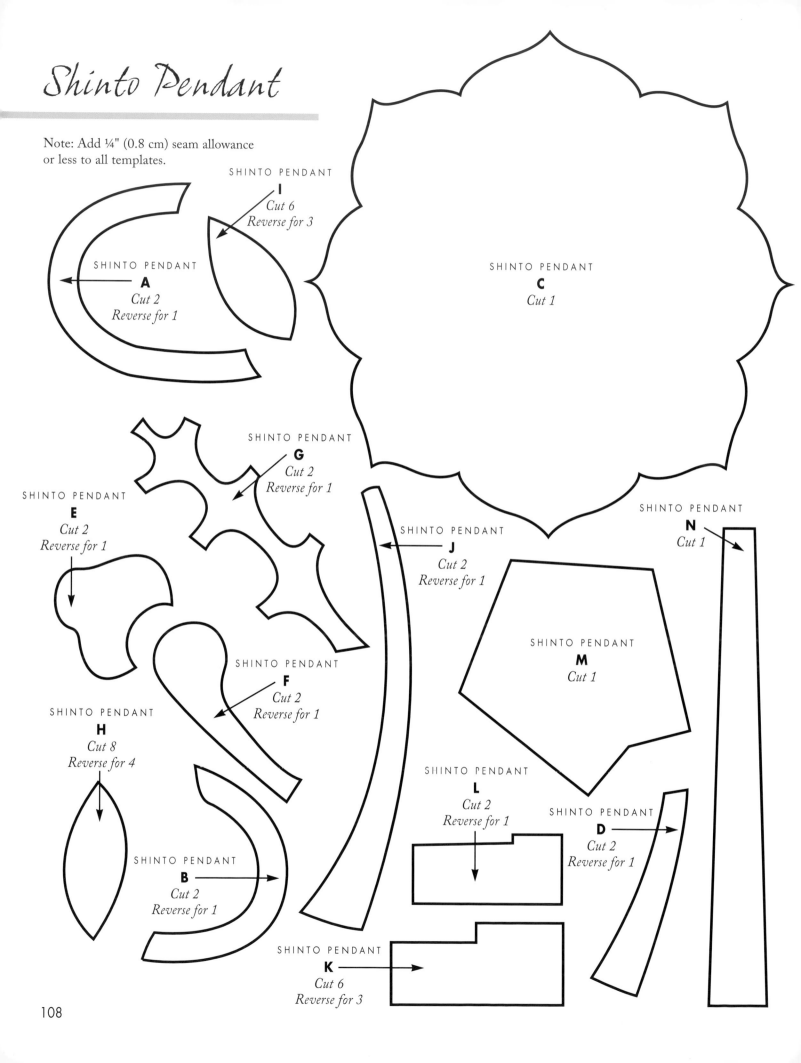

SHINTO PENDANT

I

*Cut 6
Reverse for 3*

SHINTO PENDANT

A

*Cut 2
Reverse for 1*

SHINTO PENDANT

C

Cut 1

SHINTO PENDANT

G

*Cut 2
Reverse for 1*

SHINTO PENDANT

E

*Cut 2
Reverse for 1*

SHINTO PENDANT

N

Cut 1

SHINTO PENDANT

J

*Cut 2
Reverse for 1*

SHINTO PENDANT

M

Cut 1

SHINTO PENDANT

F

*Cut 2
Reverse for 1*

SHINTO PENDANT

H

*Cut 8
Reverse for 4*

SHINTO PENDANT

L

*Cut 2
Reverse for 1*

SHINTO PENDANT

D

*Cut 2
Reverse for 1*

SHINTO PENDANT

B

*Cut 2
Reverse for 1*

SHINTO PENDANT

K

*Cut 6
Reverse for 3*

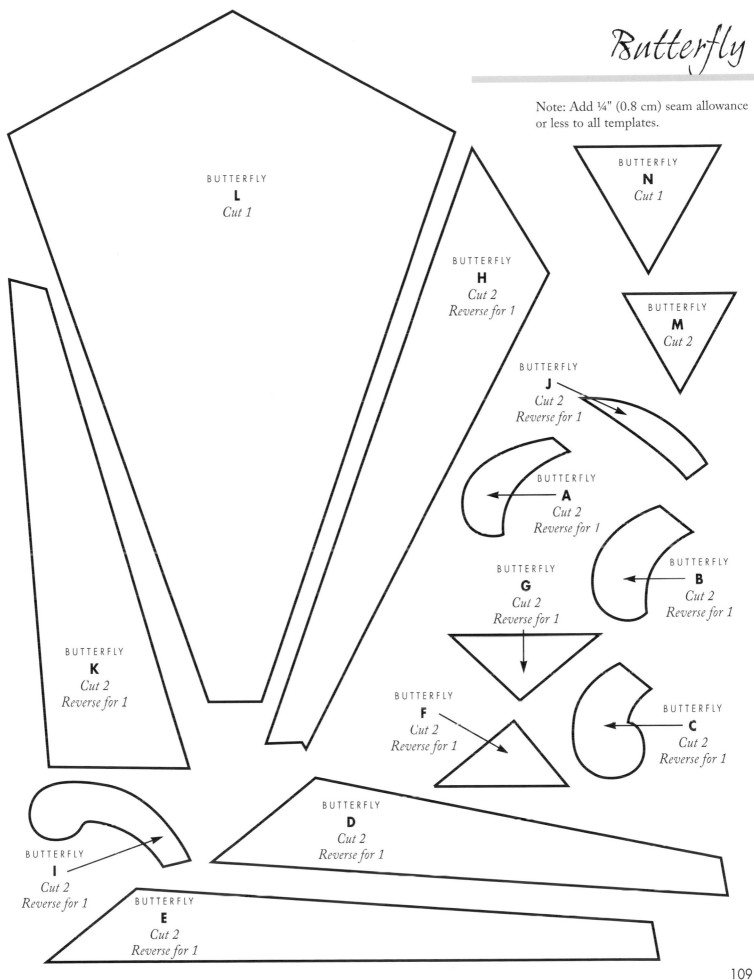

Butterfly

Note: Add ¼" (0.8 cm) seam allowance or less to all templates.

BUTTERFLY
L
Cut 1

BUTTERFLY
N
Cut 1

BUTTERFLY
H
Cut 2
Reverse for 1

BUTTERFLY
M
Cut 2

BUTTERFLY
J
Cut 2
Reverse for 1

BUTTERFLY
A
Cut 2
Reverse for 1

BUTTERFLY
B
Cut 2
Reverse for 1

BUTTERFLY
G
Cut 2
Reverse for 1

BUTTERFLY
K
Cut 2
Reverse for 1

BUTTERFLY
F
Cut 2
Reverse for 1

BUTTERFLY
C
Cut 2
Reverse for 1

BUTTERFLY
D
Cut 2
Reverse for 1

BUTTERFLY
I
Cut 2
Reverse for 1

BUTTERFLY
E
Cut 2
Reverse for 1

Lily

Note: Add ¼" (0.8 cm) seam allowance
or less to all templates.

LILY
D
Cut 1

LILY
B
Cut 1

LILY
G
Cut 1

LILY
A
Cut 1

LILY
H
Cut 1

LILY
J
Cut 1

LILY
I
Cut 1

LILY
C
Cut 1

LILY
F
Cut 1

LILY
E
Cut 1

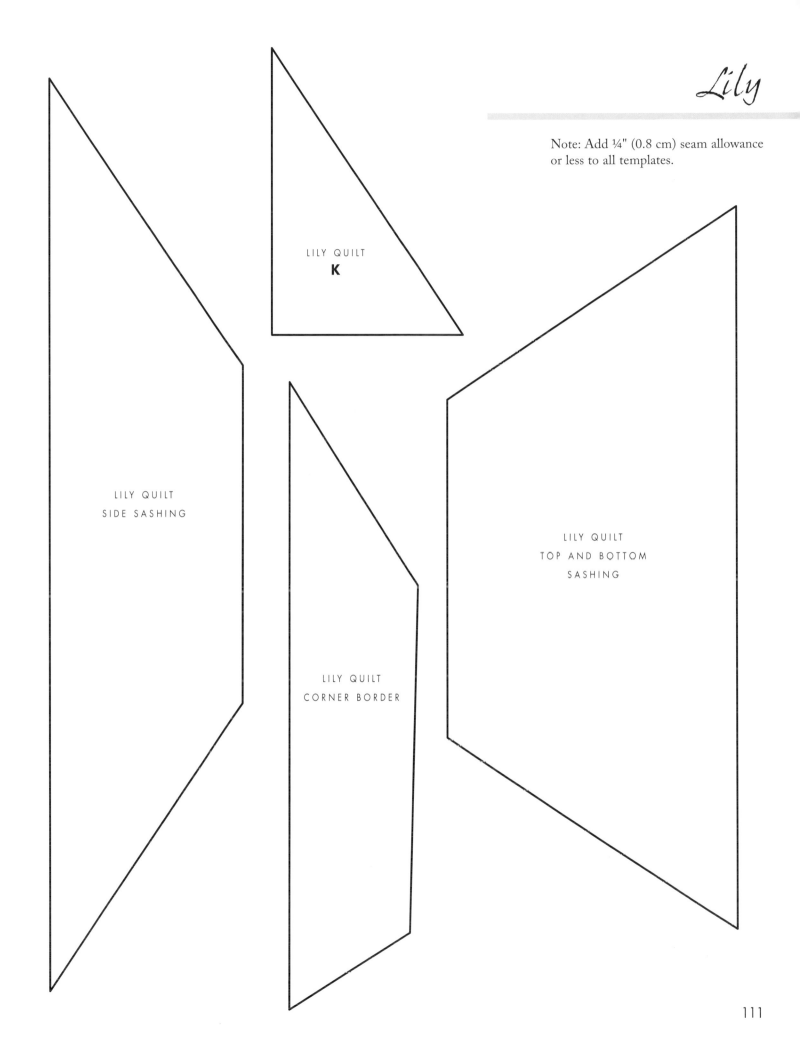

Lily

Note: Add ¼" (0.8 cm) seam allowance or less to all templates.

LILY QUILT
K

LILY QUILT
SIDE SASHING

LILY QUILT
TOP AND BOTTOM
SASHING

LILY QUILT
CORNER BORDER

Lily

Note: Add ¼"
(0.8 cm) seam
allowance or less
to all templates.

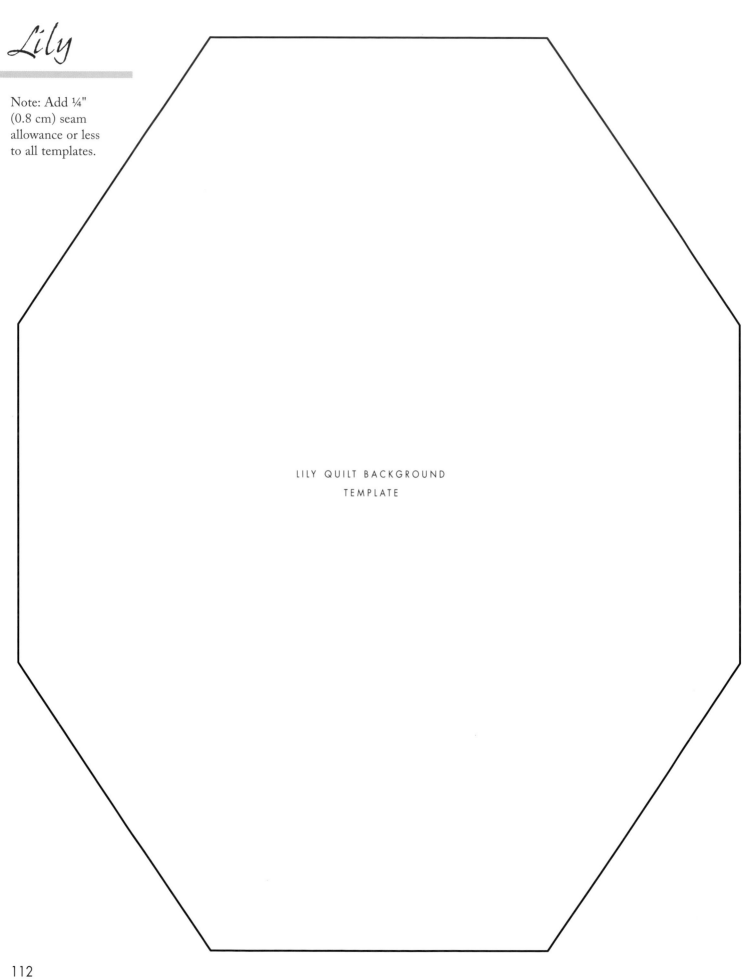

LILY QUILT BACKGROUND
TEMPLATE

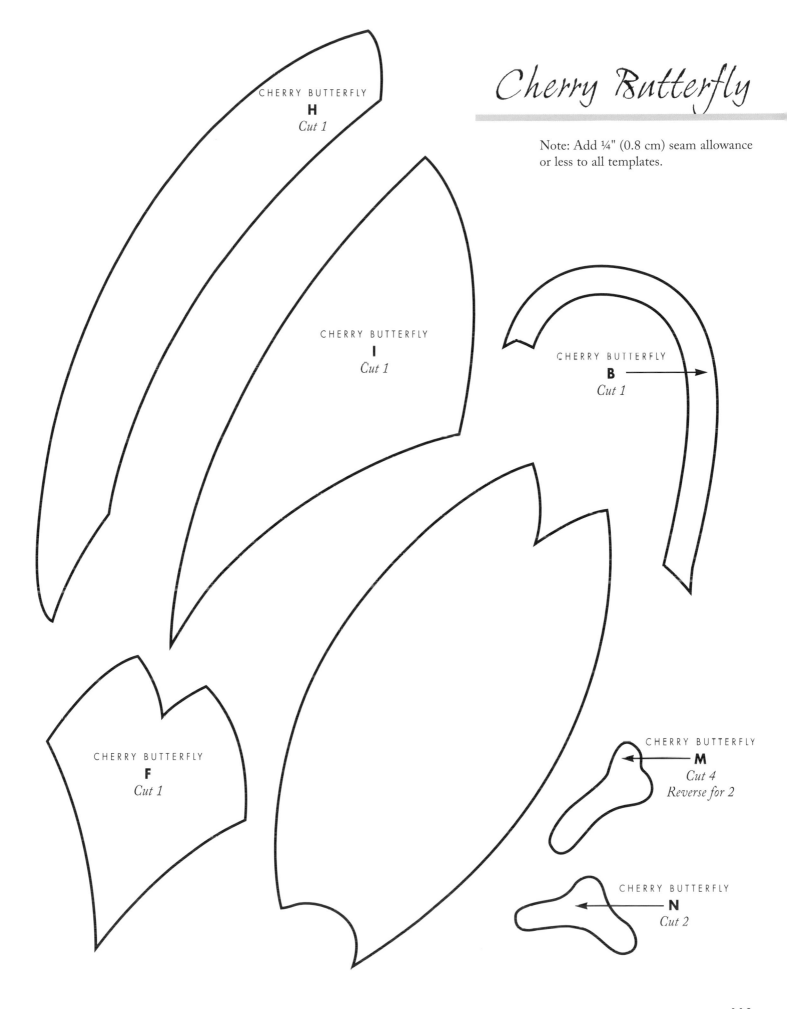

CHERRY BUTTERFLY
H
Cut 1

CHERRY BUTTERFLY
I
Cut 1

Cherry Butterfly

Note: Add ¼" (0.8 cm) seam allowance or less to all templates.

CHERRY BUTTERFLY
B
Cut 1

CHERRY BUTTERFLY
F
Cut 1

CHERRY BUTTERFLY
M
Cut 4
Reverse for 2

CHERRY BUTTERFLY
N
Cut 2

Cherry Butterfly

Note: Add ¼" (0.8 cm) seam allowance
or less to all templates.

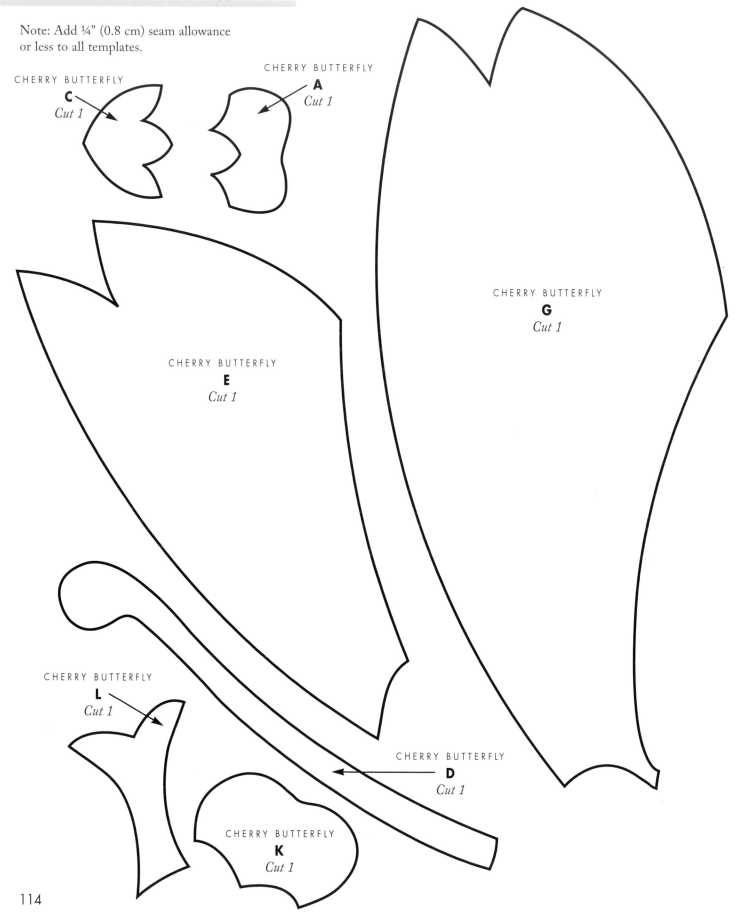

CHERRY BUTTERFLY
C
Cut 1

CHERRY BUTTERFLY
A
Cut 1

CHERRY BUTTERFLY
G
Cut 1

CHERRY BUTTERFLY
E
Cut 1

CHERRY BUTTERFLY
L
Cut 1

CHERRY BUTTERFLY
D
Cut 1

CHERRY BUTTERFLY
K
Cut 1

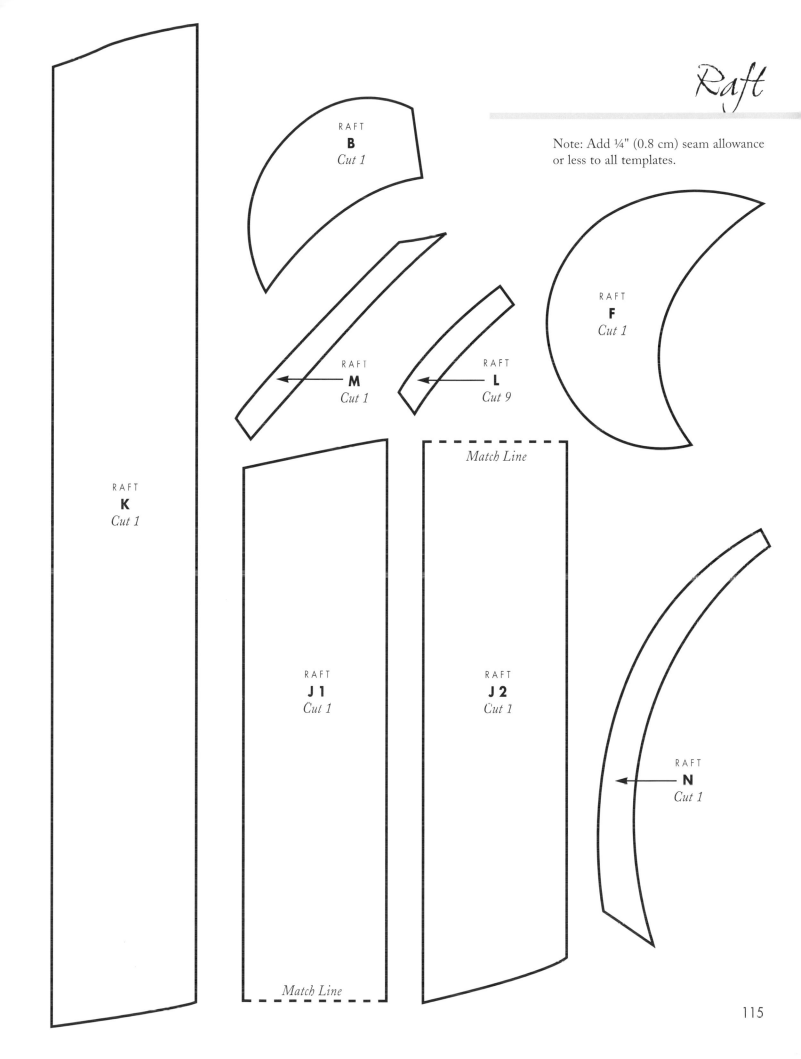

Raft

Note: Add ¼" (0.8 cm) seam allowance or less to all templates.

RAFT
B
Cut 1

RAFT
F
Cut 1

RAFT
M
Cut 1

RAFT
L
Cut 9

RAFT
K
Cut 1

Match Line

RAFT
J 1
Cut 1

RAFT
J 2
Cut 1

RAFT
N
Cut 1

Match Line

Raft

Note: Add ¼" (0.8 cm) seam allowance or less to all templates.

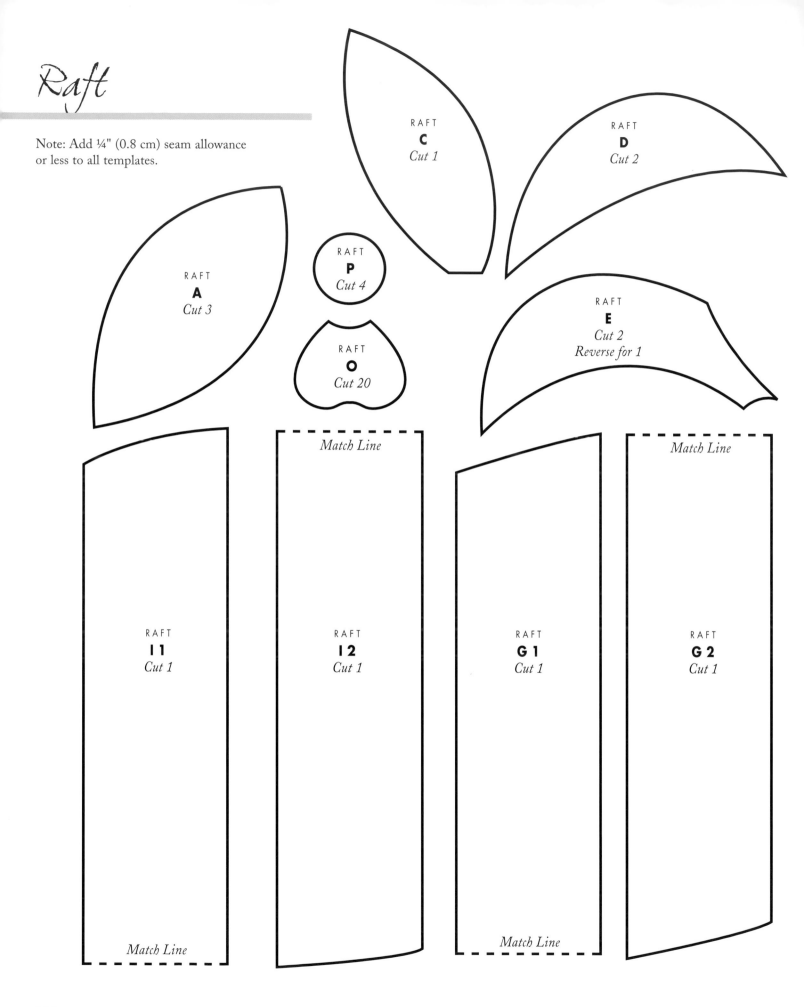

RAFT
C
Cut 1

RAFT
D
Cut 2

RAFT
A
Cut 3

RAFT
P
Cut 4

RAFT
O
Cut 20

RAFT
E
Cut 2
Reverse for 1

Match Line

RAFT
I 1
Cut 1

RAFT
I 2
Cut 1

RAFT
G 1
Cut 1

RAFT
G 2
Cut 1

Match Line

Match Line

Match Line

Note: Add ¼" (0.8 cm) seam allowance or less to all templates.

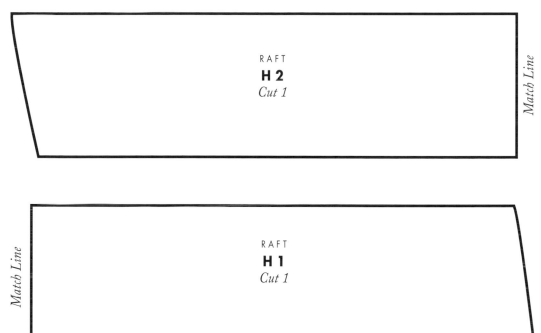

RAFT
H 2
Cut 1

Match Line

Match Line

RAFT
H 1
Cut 1

Note: Add ¼" (0.8 cm) seam allowance or less to all templates.

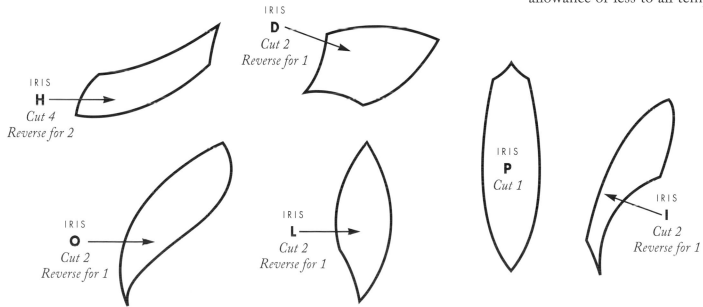

IRIS
D
Cut 2
Reverse for 1

IRIS
H
Cut 4
Reverse for 2

IRIS
O
Cut 2
Reverse for 1

IRIS
L
Cut 2
Reverse for 1

IRIS
P
Cut 1

IRIS
I
Cut 2
Reverse for 1

Iris

Note: Add ¼" (0.8 cm) seam allowance or less to all templates.

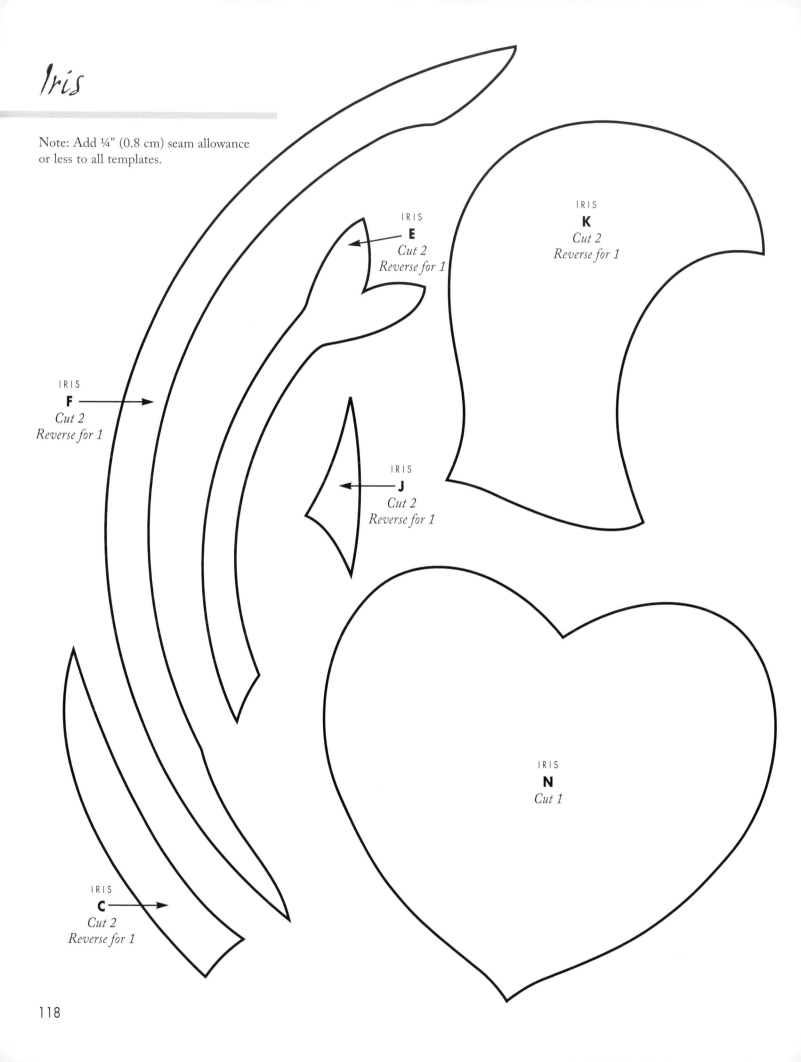

IRIS
E
Cut 2
Reverse for 1

IRIS
K
Cut 2
Reverse for 1

IRIS
F
Cut 2
Reverse for 1

IRIS
J
Cut 2
Reverse for 1

IRIS
N
Cut 1

IRIS
C
Cut 2
Reverse for 1

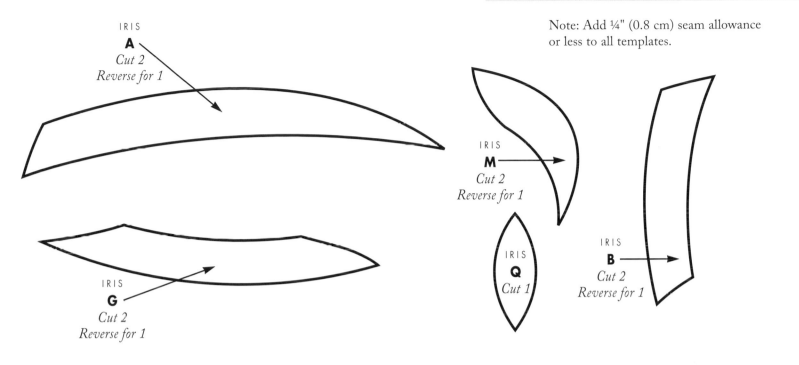

IRIS

A

Cut 2
Reverse for 1

IRIS

G

Cut 2
Reverse for 1

Note: Add ¼" (0.8 cm) seam allowance or less to all templates.

IRIS

M

Cut 2
Reverse for 1

IRIS

Q
Cut 1

IRIS

B

Cut 2
Reverse for 1

Bracken

Note: Add ¼" (0.8 cm) seam allowance or less to all templates.

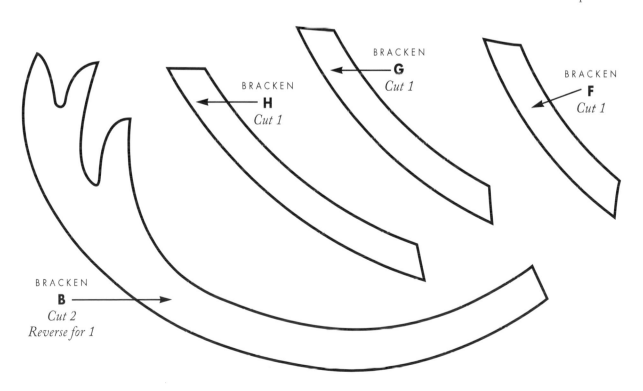

BRACKEN

H
Cut 1

BRACKEN

G
Cut 1

BRACKEN

F
Cut 1

BRACKEN

B

Cut 2
Reverse for 1

Bracken

Note: Add ¼" (0.8 cm) seam allowance or less to all templates.

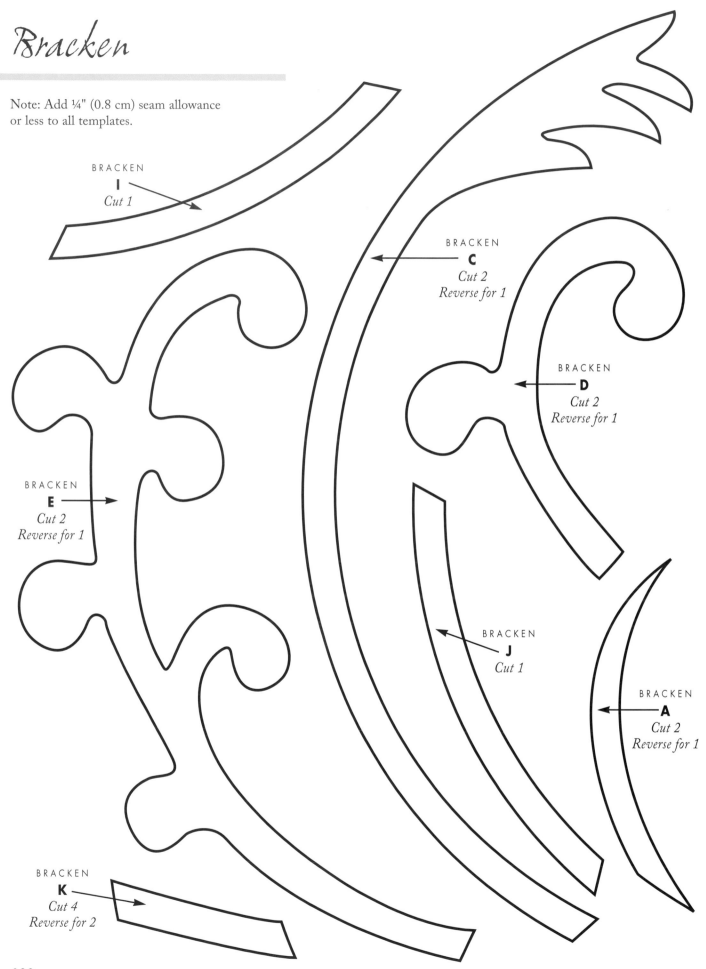

BRACKEN
I
Cut 1

BRACKEN
C
Cut 2
Reverse for 1

BRACKEN
D
Cut 2
Reverse for 1

BRACKEN
E
Cut 2
Reverse for 1

BRACKEN
J
Cut 1

BRACKEN
A
Cut 2
Reverse for 1

BRACKEN
K
Cut 4
Reverse for 2

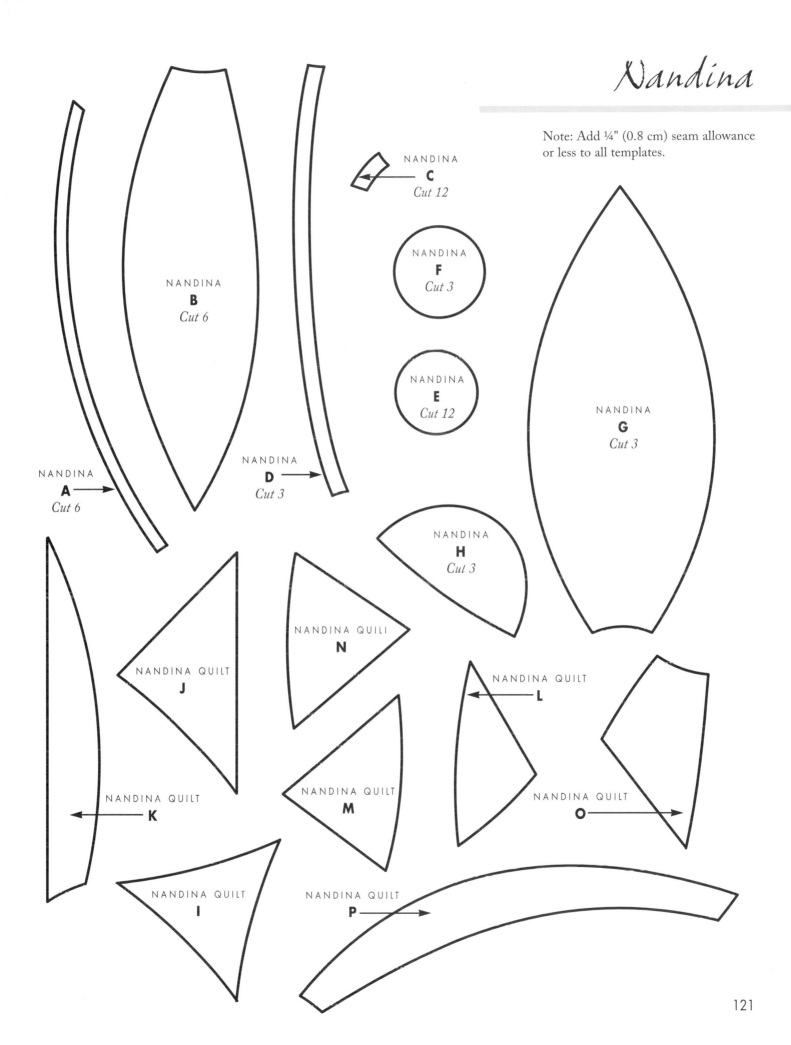

Nandina

Note: Add ¼" (0.8 cm) seam allowance or less to all templates.

NANDINA
C
Cut 12

NANDINA
F
Cut 3

NANDINA
E
Cut 12

NANDINA
B
Cut 6

NANDINA
G
Cut 3

NANDINA
A
Cut 6

NANDINA
D
Cut 3

NANDINA
H
Cut 3

NANDINA QUILT
J

NANDINA QUILT
N

NANDINA QUILT
L

NANDINA QUILT
K

NANDINA QUILT
M

NANDINA QUILT
O

NANDINA QUILT
I

NANDINA QUILT
P

Lesson Plans

Supply List for Each Workshop

- Fabric for the quilt top
- Backing fabric
- Batting
- Sewing and quilting needles
- Sewing and quilting thread
- Thimble
- Straight pins
- Ruler
- Paper and fabric scissors
- Tracing paper
- Template plastic
- Pencil
- Colored pencils
- Fabric marker (or pencil)
- White drawing paper
- Notebook

Suggestions for a Half-Day Workshop

Making a Single Block: *Noshi*
(For Beginning and Intermediate Quilters)

During this sample lesson, students will make one of the easier blocks in this book. The process includes learning and practicing a method of appliqué and looking at color and pattern in fabrics in a new way.

First Hour

Give each student one or more photocopies of the diagram for the *Noshi* block (page 44). Discuss color selection and placement in the block: contrast of light and dark colors, texture, movement, and use of bold fabric and large design. Instruct students to experiment with color by coloring their photocopies and then making their final choices on colors they will use. Students select background fabric and cut out the background square, following the lengthwise grain or the print of the fabric pattern. Following the diagram on page 44, students lightly draw the outlines of the pattern onto the fabric using a pencil or fabric marker. Discuss with students the type of fabric to be used for the project.

Second Hour

Students select the fabrics that they will need to match their color sketches as closely as possible. They cut all the fabric pieces using the templates, following the lengthwise grain or the print of the fabric patterns. Students then pin and appliqué pattern pieces to the background square in the sequence shown on page 44.

Third Hour

Discuss with students how they will select other patterns or other fabrics to complete a four-block lap quilt at home. Demonstrate how to join the four blocks into a quilt top, and add batting and quilt backing. Demonstrate how to quilt following the seamlines or in a design of your choice.

Suggestions for an Extended Classroom Schedule

Making a More Complex Design: *Gingko* Block or Quilt
(For Intermediate and Advanced Quilters)

These are ideas to be incorporated into a course for teaching experienced quilters how to refine their appliqué skills and to gain further confidence. The course is based on a design that includes many curved seams. It also includes suggestions for those who wish to encourage students to create their own curved-line appliqué designs. Feel free to use these ideas along with your own teaching experience to modify the course as you wish.

Using the *Gingko* design on page 30, begin by instructing students to make the block following the instructions and the procedure outlined in the earlier lesson. Students may make and finish just one block or the full quilt.

Demonstrate the appliqué technique used in this design. You may also wish to demonstrate other techniques for piecing curved seams and other forms of appliqué.

Discuss the use of color in the project. Kumiko has made wonderful use of contrasting colors. Have students experiment with different colors and see how the image changes. If your students are making the quilt, let them try rearranging the templates for different effects.

Students who have created new designs can form small groups and share their ideas. Conduct an open discussion about the pros and cons of each design.

Bibliography

The Art Institute of Chicago, *Museum Studies: Asian Art*. The Art Institute of Chicago, Chicago. 1996.

DeMente, Boye, *Everything Japanese: The Authoritative Reference on Japan Today*. Passport Books, a division of NTC/Contemporary Publishing Company, Lincolnwood, Illinois. 1992.

Dower, John W., *The Elements of Japanese Design: A Handbook of Family Crests, Heraldry & Symbolism, with over 2,700 crests drawn by Kiyoshi Kawamoto*. Walker/Weatherhill. New York, Tokyo. First edition, 1971. First paperback edition, 1990. The editors of *Circles of the East* owe a great debt to John W. Dower. Although many texts were consulted for the writing of the introduction to this book, it was Dr. Dower's work to which we returned again and again; his understanding of the role of crests in Japanese history is unparalleled. *The Elements of Japanese Design* not only offers a wealth of information, but is both visually and intellectually stimulating.

Friar, Stephen and Ferguson, John, *Basic Heraldry*. W.W. Norton and Company, New York and London. 1993.

Grosswirth, Marvin, *The Heraldry Book: A Guide to Designing Your Own Coat of Arms*. Doubleday & Co., Garden City, New York. 1981.

Lehner, Ernst and Lehner, Johanna, *Folklore and Symbolism of Flowers, Plants, and Trees*. Tudor Publishing Company, New York. 1960.

Mahoney, Jean and Rao, Peggy Landers, *At Home with Japanese Design*. Shufunotomo Co. Ltd., Tokyo. 1990.

Montdveiffe, Iain and Pottinger, Don, *Simple Heraldry, Cheerfully Illustrated*. Thos. Nelson & Sons, Ltd. London, 1967.

Neubecker, Ottfried, *A Guide to Heraldry*. McGraw-Hill Book Co. Ltd., Maidenhead, England. 1979.

Okada, Yuzuru, *Japanese Family Crests*. Board of Tourist Industry, Japanese Government Railways. 1941.

Ulak, James T., *Japanese Prints*. Abbeville Publishing Group, New York. 1995.

Woodcock, Thomas, and Robinson, John Martin, *The Oxford Guide to Heraldry*. Oxford University Press, Oxford, New York, Melbourne, Toronto. 1988.

Zieber, Eugene, *Heraldry in America*. Haskell House Publishers Ltd. New York. 1969.

. . . *Japanese Design Motifs: 4260 Illustrations of Heraldic Crests*, compiled by the Matsuya Piece-Goods Store. Translated, and with a new introduction, by Fumie Adachi. Dover Publications, Inc. New York. Copyright 1972. Originally published in Japan c. 1913.

. . . *Japanese Emblems and Designs*. Edited by Walter Amstutz, with an introduction by J. Hillier. University of Toronto Press, Toronto 5, Canada and Amstutz De Clivo Press, Talaker 41, 8001 Zurich. Copyright 1970 by Amstutz De Clivo Press.

. . . *Kodansha Enclyclopedia of Japan, Volume 2*. Kodansha Ltd., Tokyo and New York. 1983.

About the Author

Kumiko Sudo is an internationally acclaimed fiber artist. Before moving to the United States in 1985, she was known by quilters throughout Japan for her teaching of quilting and other fiber arts on Japanese national television. Kumiko's work is today known and respected worldwide, and her quilts are in several fine public and private collections, including the Museum of American Folk Art in New York and the University of Oregon Museum of Art. Kumiko's books have inspired quilters and fiber artists all over the world and include bestseller *Fabled Flowers*, *East Quilts West*, *East Quilts West II* and *Expressive Quilts*.

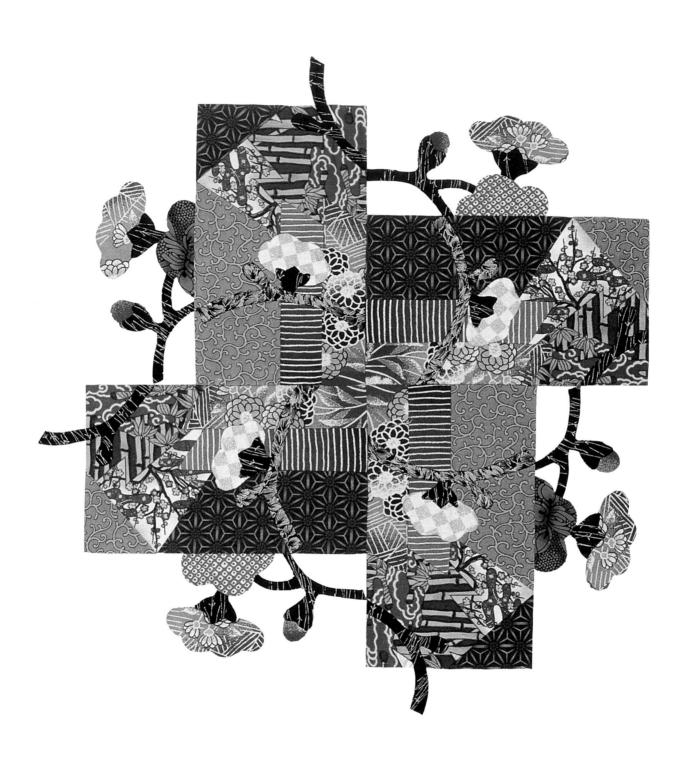

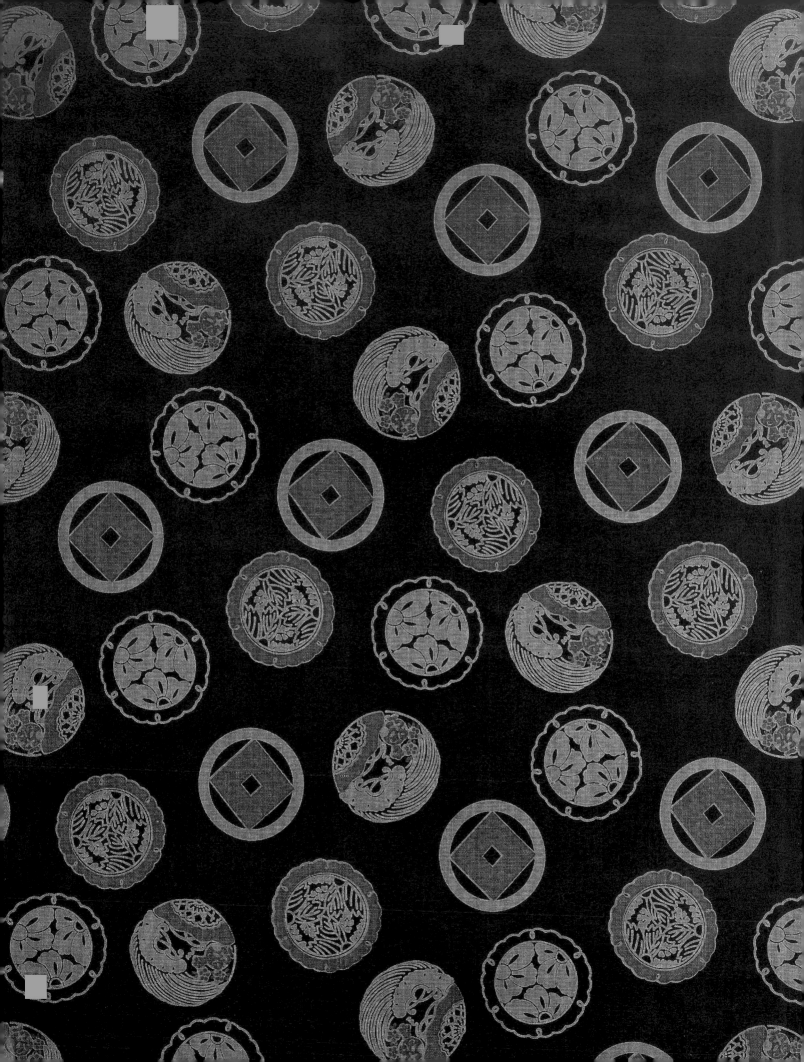